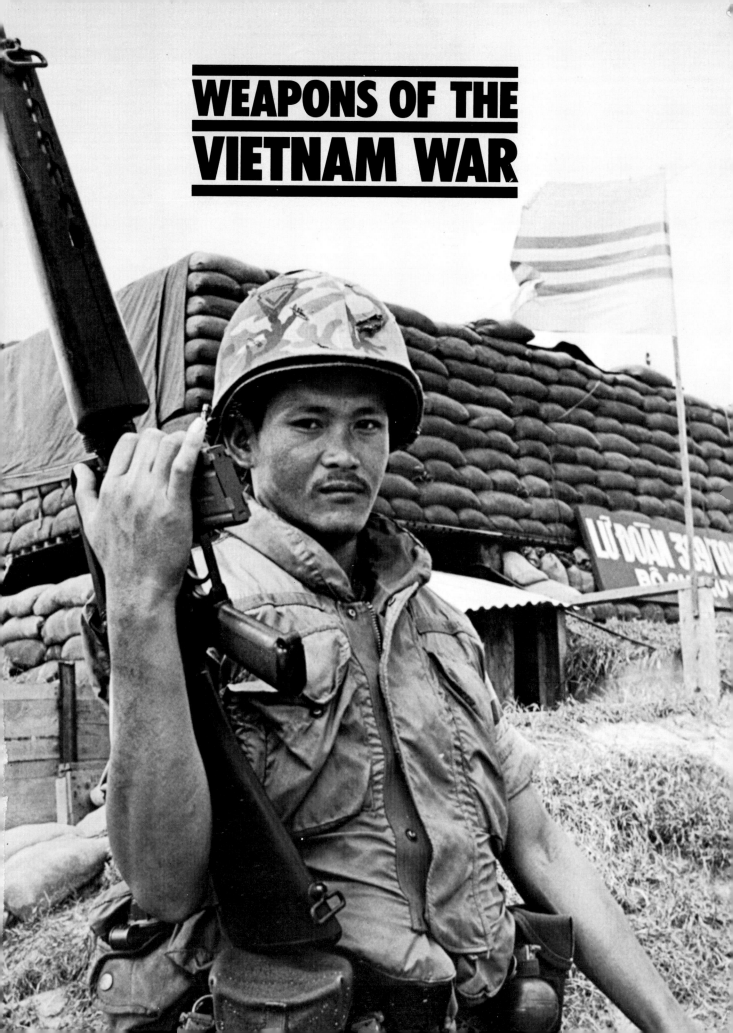

WEAPONS OF THE VIETNAM WAR

WEAPONS OF THE VIETNAM WAR

ANTHONY ROBINSON
ANTONY PRESTON
IAN V. HOGG

GALLERY BOOKS
An imprint of W.H. Smith Publishers Inc.
112 Madison Avenue
New York, New York 10016

A Bison Book

Published by Gallery Books
A Division of W. H. Smith Publishers Inc.
112 Madison Avenue
New York, New York 10016

Produced by
Bison Books Corp.
17 Sherwood Place
Greenwich, CT 06830
USA

Printed in Hong Kong

2 3 4 5 6 7 8 9 10

ISBN 0-8317-9382-1

Page 1: A South Vietnamese Marine guards a
bunker complex near the city of Quang Tri in
February 1972.

Pages 2/3: A Lockheed AC-130A fires its
side-mounted 20mm Vulcan multi-barrel
cannon.

Pages 4/5: UH-1D 'Huey' helicopters lift off
after landing members of the 1st ARVN
Division in the A Shau Valley in 1968.

CONTENTS

GUERILLA
WARFARE

At the outset, it is as well to bear in mind that guerilla warfare is not a twentieth century innovation, nor, in spite of some of the most-publicized writers on the subject, is it an invention of Marxist origin. Guerilla warfare is defined in the dictionary as "an irregular mode of carrying out war by the constant attacks of independent bands" and there are innumerable examples of this form of warfare extending back into Biblical times. The name appeared during the Peninsular War, when Napoleon's occupation of Spain was violently opposed by the Spanish who proceeded to fight a 'guerilla' or 'little war' against his armies with considerable success.

The Viet Cong operations in Vietnam were guerilla warfare insofar as they involved 'constant attacks of independent bands', but in fact the VC forces were an organized army rather than a collection of irregular groups. But, although the military operations began under French rule in 1946, the intentions of the Viet Minh (who fought the French) and the Viet Cong (who continued the war after the French had departed) were totally different. The Viet Minh were intent upon evicting a colonial power and ruling their country themselves; the Viet Cong had no colonial power to evict, and were solely concerned with seizing power for themselves. But by skilful propaganda the Viet Cong were able to in-

herit the mantle of the Viet Minh and so claim that their objective was nationalist rather than communist.

After the Geneva Agreements of 1954 some 30,000 South Vietnamese troops who had fought with the Viet Minh chose to go to North Vietnam and join forces with the Communists there. Over the next few years they were assiduously trained in the basic techniques of guerilla warfare; some were additionally trained as weapons instructors, political instructors, explosives experts, radio technicians, any and every craft which might be required in setting up and maintaining a subversive network throughout South Vietnam. Once trained to the satisfaction of their mentors, they were infiltrated across the border and returned to their native district, often to their families, and by about 1963 they had all crossed the border and were in place. But long before that the civil war within South Vietnam had begun, and it was the sub-structure set up by these infiltrated agents which formed the supportive element for the fierce guerilla activity.

The fight in Vietnam was formally called a 'People's Revolutionary War' and had significant differences from the norm of guerilla warfare, which is normally considered to be the use of irregulars to harass an invading or occupying force. It was this type of war which was

waged by Tito's forces in Yugoslavia, against the occupying German Army, and by Russian partisans against the invading German Army. Whilst guerilla operations of this sort have often made life extremely difficult for the occupier or invader, and have frequently played a major part in his eventual defeat, it is rarely that guerilla actions have been completely and independently successful. Moreover, it is axiomatic that guerillas can never achieve success against a determined regular force who are prepared to fight fire with fire; no totalitarian army is ever likely to be more than inconvenienced by guerillas, whereas the armies of democratic states can rarely defeat them, since such states simply do not have the stomach for the violent repressive action necessary. But, irrespective of this aspect, guerilla warfare wins by obtaining military decisions.

A 'People's Revolutionary War' however, does not have a military decision as its end purpose, but a political takeover. So that in addition to guerilla warfare as a tactic, it also requires a political strategy in which it builds up an alternative, revolutionary, government and obtains popular support to the point where the alternative can challenge the existing government for control of the country. To achieve this end the campaign can be said to divide into three

phases; the build-up during which the clandestine sub-structure is prepared and the 'troops' trained and positioned; the guerilla phase in which open warfare breaks out and is maintained until the revolutionary force is as strong as or stronger than the existing government; and the consolidation phase when it exerts a final offensive and takes over the country.

In Vietnam the first phase began in the 1930s with the first Viet Minh reaction to French rule; it was nurtured and expanded during the war years by patriotic activity against the occupying Japanese, and turned into the second and third phases in 1945-54 with the war against the French. So far as the Viet Cong were concerned, though, this was merely the first phase, and they were able to resuscitate many dormant organizations much more easily than would have been the case had they been forced to start completely from scratch. The second war, that of the Viet Cong against the South

Overleaf: Fires rage following a Viet Cong rocket attack on Da Nang air base.

Above left: The victorious Viet Minh take stock of their war booty after the Battle of Dien Bien Phu in May 1954.

Left: Viet Minh troops receive a hero's welcome at Hong Gay in August 1955.

Below: French troops move against enemy positions around Dien Bien Phu.

Vietnamese government, was therefore able to build on the work of the Viet Minh and move into its second phase very rapidly.

There are three more factors which need to be considered; time, space and cost. These are the keys to Revolutionary War. Time means little to dedicated revolutionaries; if they do not succeed, then their children or their grandchildren will. This is one reason why revolutionary movements always aim at recruiting the young students and workers, in the hope that they will henceforth dedicate their lives to the movement. Time is necessary to build up the first phase of the strategy, to recruit, train and infiltrate agents, to build up a cohesive network of sympathizers, agents, spies, suppliers, couriers, 'safe houses' and all the other clandestine substructure. Time is necessary to weather reverses; if the commander enters the guerilla phase too soon, he must withdraw again and let the entire movement become dormant, perhaps for several years, until his network is again built up, until he has sufficient forces and weapons, until the time is politically ripe to try once more.

Space is necessary in which to live and operate, and it also helps to buy time. The beginning of a revolutionary movement will have the forces concealed in wild country, mountains or jungles, where government forces never go and are unlikely, therefore, to discover the guerillas. Gradually they expand their influence, over a village, a group of villages, a county, a province, and as they gain space for movement in this way they also gain more time in which to operate successfully. In the classic pattern the revolution begins in the remotest areas, expands, and then, with the country as its firm base, it begins to flow around the urban centers. Performed carefully, a revolutionary movement can control a massive area of country, and, more important, control the occupants, before the government forces take alarm. Space also gives the guerilla movement an enlarged recruiting base and thus ensures a plentiful supply of troops.

In the matter of cost, guerillas and revolutionaries use a different currency to regular forces. The currency of guerillas is manpower, not money. No guerilla force can hope to succeed unless it has outside assistance, generally in the form of a major power which has a political aim in view; in the case of Vietnam it was the Communist bloc as represented by Russia on the one hand and China on the other. Both these provided weapons to the revolutionary force, and in the initial stages these were the most basic types of weapons – rifles, grenades, submachine guns, explosives – which, since both these nations had immense reserve stocks of wartime weapons, represented a minimal financial outlay. The guerilla does not have an enormous logistic 'tail' as does a regular army, no immense workshops, supply columns, administrative units, and therefore the need for money is minimal. Their uniform is basic, their medical and food requirements are largely met by local provision by sympathisers, what else they need can frequently be stolen from the government forces.

What they must, in the initial stages, hoard is manpower. When the movement begins it must be careful not to mount military operations which are hazardous, since it cannot afford casualties; there are but a few trained men and these must be safeguarded. Operations will take place two or three times a year, and then only against easy targets. Success breeds confidence, and provides recruits; these must then be trained by the existing guerillas. And so it is only after a guerilla movement has been in force for some years and has built up a sizeable stock of manpower, that it can become more bold in its military ventures.

Had the war in Vietnam remained at that sort of level, it is doubtful whether the Viet Cong would have achieved victory at all. But when the third phase, that of the all-out offensive to take control of the country, came within sight it was complicated by the arrival of the Americans, who had upset the balance. As a result, the North Vietnamese Army joined the fight, more 'currency' became available and military operations suddenly became feasible even when they suffered high casualty rates. Once this additional force was made available, the end was rarely in doubt, since the

Below: The corpse of a Viet Cong killed during the fighting of the Tet offensive is displayed beside his weapons.

Above: Vietnamese peasants rush to board a Marine Corps CH-46 helicopter, which will evacuate them to a safer area.

population base of North Vietnam was capable of supplying half a million recruits a year, far more than the South Vietnamese or Americans were willing to put into the fight. By expending manpower, of which they had virtually a limitless supply, the Viet Cong imposed a situation which the Americans and South Vietnamese could only meet by money and manpower, and in neither country were the citizenry willing to foot the bill.

Much of the expertise in guerilla warfare which the Viet Cong had in their early days was a legacy from the war in China. When the Second World War broke out most of the Vietnamese Communist leaders were in China and they formed guerilla bands to operate with the Kuomintang against the Japanese. These bands were principally concerned with collecting information to feed back to regular KMT units, though one active

guerilla force under Giap was set up in the north of Vietnam close to the Chinese border. This called itself the 'Army of Propaganda and Liberation', but since there were few Japanese or French forces in the area it did little military work, but much political propaganda, and by the end of the war it controlled a considerable area. In the confused situation after the Japanese surrender the Communists were the only organized group in a political vacuum, and they rapidly gained control of North Vietnam in a near-bloodless revolution. They seized vast quantities of arms and were also supplied with weapons from Nationalist China and by way of American supplies dropped by air to the guerillas during the war. In the ten months before the French were able to return in some military strength, the Communists were able to secrete these weapons in hides, build up their substructure and train their guerilla forces unhindered.

In December 1946 Viet Minh forces opened the war against the French, us-

ing the traditional guerilla methods; mining roads and railways, blowing up bridges, ambushing patrols and convoys, assassinating these of the wrong political hue and making short attacks on French police and patrol posts. By making pin-prick attacks they would draw the French forces, never numerically great, further and further from their bases so that they could attack their supply lines. Every time the French made an attack, the guerillas would melt away and re-form some miles further on. Eventually the French would realize that they were too far from their bases for comfort and would retreat, followed and harassed every step of the way by the guerillas.

By 1950 Giap had built up a sufficiently numerous force for him to commit whole units into battle; indeed he was now commanding a regular army, not merely a collection of guerilla bands. Using these regular forces he made head-on attacks against French garrisons, and he received several severe defeats. He returned to guerilla tactics again, mobile

bands who made brief sorties and retired into their jungle or mountain enclaves, and against this form of warfare the French could make no headway. Eventually, in 1954, the French sued for peace and Giap had won control of North Vietnam.

From then until 1960 there was peace of a sort in South Vietnam while Giap 'inserted' his infiltrators. Guerilla warfare began to make itself felt from about 1957 onward. One tactic was the systematic assassination of village leaders, teachers, land-owners and similar 'dangerous elements'; by 1959 about two-thirds of this class had been eliminated throughout South Vietnam. This effectively removed any informed opposition to the Communists among the villagers and more or less consolidated the agrarian base.

The next move was to carry the war to the military forces of South Vietnam by means of raids and ambushes, and it soon became apparent that the ARVN had little stomach for fighting; this was particularly noted by the Viet Cong after the Battle of Ap Bac in January 1963. In this battle a large force of South Vietnamese armored infantry set out to seek

some Viet Cong and found 200 of them well-sited along a canal bank. It was subsequently discovered that the VC were well aware of the approach of the ARVN and had decided to make a stand in order to gauge what sort of opposition they were likely to come up against in the future. The ARVN had some 2000 troops, armored personnel carriers, helicopters and even South Vietnamese paratroops at their disposal, but inept tactics, poor handling of men and equipment, and failure to heed the advice of American advisers led to severe casualties and after giving the ARVN a bloody nose, the Viet Cong evaporated into the countryside during the night, leaving the ARVN force to deliver a cumbersome attack against an empty position. This battle gave the VC a considerable morale boost and led them to become more adventurous in their attacks.

The arrival of American forces, with better equipment, better training and better tactics was something of a setback but, as with Giap in 1950, it merely meant trading time for space. Instead of pursuing major attacks, as they had been doing against the ARVN, the guerillas now pulled back and reverted to their

former techniques of small-group raids, ambushes, bridge demolitions, mining and all the traditional activities. Doing this allowed them to gauge the response of the Americans, sound out their tactics, and discover their techniques. Once this was done, the big groups came back into being and began making attacks on fire bases, major ambushes and, eventually, pitched battles.

Guerilla operations varied from simple disruptive pin-pricks by individuals or small teams, all the way up to formal operations conforming in all respects to operations of a regular army. At the lowest level the individual guerillas living in or near a village would keep up a constant pressure on American or ARVN forces in their neighborhood by setting booby-traps and sniping. Some traps required little technology in their preparation; such simple but lethal devices as pitfalls and snares could be made from natural materials which were readily to hand in the jungle or scrub, the only difficult part being to disguise the trap so that the victim never saw it until he was in it. The 'panji stick' was the simplest device and lent itself to innumerable variations. In its oldest form (for it had been used as an animal trap for hundreds of years) the panji stick was a stake of sharpened bamboo which had been hardened in a fire. A pit would be dug in a jungle track, its size depending upon the objective; it could be large enough for a man to fall into, or merely deep enough to allow a man's foot to drop into it. At the bottom of the pit a number of panji stakes would be emplaced, their butt ends buried in the ground and the sharp tips pointing upwards. The pit was then covered with vines, thin sticks and leaves until it was invisible. When the victim trod on the covering, he pitched through it; a man-trap would cause him to be impaled on the panji tips. A smaller trap would allow him to tread with sufficient weight that the panji pierced the sole of his boot and impaled his foot. A variation was to line the edges of the pit with panjis inclined downwards, so that they trapped the foot and prevented the

Above: A lance corporal of the 5th Marines examines a rifle captured from the Viet Cong at Cai Dong in August 1966.
Left: Men of the 101st Airborne Division examine a VC cache of B-41 (RPG-7) and B-40 rockets captured in August 1968.

man withdrawing it; held in this position he was an easy target for a sniper. It was not unknown for the tips of the panji to be smeared with excreta or rotted animal flesh in order to infect the wound.

Another simple trick was to take a number of short panji and embed them in a ball of mud, which was then hardened in the sun. This ball was then suspended by a vine rope and pulled to one side of a track, where it was anchored against a tree by some form of quick-release. A trip wire across the track controlled the release of the mud ball, so that when the victim caught the trip wire in his boot, the heavy ball would swing out of the trees and smash into his side, inflicting serious wounds.

Equally primitive was the bow and arrow, not used as a hand weapon but emplaced in a tree or in a pit alongside the trail, the bow drawn and the arrow fitted in place, and the whole contrivance controlled by another trip wire and quick release device. As with the panji, this trap had its origins with the aboriginal tribes of the highlands, who had used it for generations as an animal trap.

If explosives were available, then the booby-trap options widened considerably. One of the most effective was the technique of fastening a tin can (old American C-ration cans were ideally proportioned for this) to a tree alongside the trail and inserting a hand grenade with a cord tied to it. As the grenade went into the can, its actuating lever was confined by the body of the can, and the safety pin could be withdrawn. The cord was then stretched across the track and tied to another tree, and the grenade and can concealed by a scattering of leaves. As soon as someone tripped over the

cord, the grenade was jerked from the can and on to the track, the lever was released, and a few seconds later the grenade would detonate. Where grenades were in ample supply it was possible to put a can and grenade at each side of the track and simply tie the cord between the two grenades, so that the victim withdrew both and ensured a detonation on each side of himself.

The ability of grenades to function under water with reliability was soon realized to be a valuable aid to trapping. In the Mekong Delta and other areas in which government forces would frequently use streams as their routes, a grenade would be tied to a peg hammered into the stream bed or bank below the water line. A cord ran across the stream from the grenade's safety pin to

another peg. As the victim waded up the stream he would pull the cord, releasing the pin and detonating the grenade.

One of the problems confronting the first guerillas was that of obtaining a firearm with which to fight. The classic method is, of course, to obtain them from the enemy – in this case the South Vietnamese regular troops – but this involves killing or wounding the owner before he is likely to part with the gun. To manage this, the Viet Minh and Viet Cong turned to home-made weapons in considerable numbers. These ranged from shotguns made from water-pipes, through one-shot pistols, to relatively complex copies of western weapons. They were made in jungle and village workshops, usually run by one man who had some engineering ability together with a 'staff' of apprentices who could be relied upon to perform one specific task – filing, drilling, shaping or assembly – reliably. One simple conversion was done by obtaining old and worn-out French rifles and converting them to .410-gauge shotguns, a weapon which demanded less accuracy than a rifle and was amply lethal at short range. Handguns could be made from scrap pipe, a simple breech made from a door-bolt, and a firing pin made from a nail, propelled by a rubber band.

All these weapons were made from totally inadequate materials; the metal was soft and was never heat-treated, barrels were rarely rifled, and the clearances between the component parts was, by gunsmith standards, enormous. But they were all capable of firing one or two shots before they disintegrated, and this was all that was required of them. Armed with a home-made gun the guerilla would prepare a panji pit and lie in wait alongside the trail until an ARVN soldier put his foot in it; he then stepped in close and fired, grabbed the soldier's rifle or submachine gun, and took to the jungle. The home-made gun, if it was still fit to be fired, was then passed down the chain of seniority to the next junior guerilla, who was then at liberty to go out and repeat the performance and obtain his own weapon.

Left: A booby trap intended to catch the VC was set by a Civilian Irregular Defense Guard in Tay Ninh Province.

The captured gun would be used as long as ammunition was available or until it developed some defect. When that happened it was frequently taken to the village workshop and converted so as to obtain an extra lease of life from it. US semi-automatic carbines which had broken down would be converted into single-shot bolt action rifles, sometimes being chambered for another cartridge which was in more ample supply. If the weapon was beyond such conversion, then it would be dismantled and the us-

Right: A typical VC booby trap was this mace formed by a 200lb ball of hardened mud imbedded with panji stakes. Hung to the side of a trail and activated by a trip wire, it could cause severe wounds.

Below: A display of captured VC arms.

Left: An American soldier emerges from a VC tunnel entrance after investigating the underground complex – a dirty and often dangerous undertaking.

Above: A Marine and his scout dog check out a VC bunker near Hoi An.

able parts salvaged for incorporation into a home-made design. There was no end to this ingenuity and many military museums throughout the world now have interesting examples of Viet Minh and Viet Cong home-made weapons.

The home-made weapons flourished from the immediate postwar period until about 1963, at which time the supply of Soviet and Chinese manufactured Kalashnikov automatic rifles began to flow; by 1967 the home-made guns had almost entirely disappeared, and the AK47 became the standard guerilla weapon.

Once firearms were available the guerillas were ready to progress from individual actions to group actions, and their principal tactic was the ambush.

A properly conducted ambush is a precise operation requiring forethought,

planning and discipline, and it was fortunate for the US and ARVN soldiers that these are the very attributes which guerillas rarely possess. The site for the ambush must first be selected and carefully reconnoitered; it should permit the ambush party to approach unseen, and retreat under cover; it should allow them ample fields of fire which do not endanger their own party; it should be so located that the victims are constrained into the ambush area by natural features – streams, cliffs, valleys or even walls and buildings. The position and function of every man and weapon in the ambush party must be planned and thoroughly understood, and the exact course of action to be followed by each man must also be laid down. The actions to be taken in the event of various responses by the enemy must be foreseen and planned for, as must the actions at the end of the successful ambush. Only when all this has been done does the ambush party set out.

Once in place, and this may be done several hours before the victims are ex-

pected, the ambush party melts into the countryside and vanishes from sight and sound. There is no smoking, chattering, eating or drinking, no movement of any sort. Once the victims appear the front and rear of their party are attacked simultaneously; if the victims are a vehicle column this means setting the first and last vehicles ablaze so as to block the route forward or back for the remainder of the party and keep them trapped in the killing zone. Thereafter the ambush party pick their assigned targets and fire until they are defeated; this man may be told to fire at any officer, recognizable perhaps by his pistol; that man to attack any radio vehicle, recognizable by its antenna; another man to throw grenades into the back of vehicles, another to engage any armored vehicle with his rocket launcher. What should not happen is that all the ambush party stand up and blaze away in all directions in the best Hollywood manner.

This, however, is what often happened with Viet Cong ambushes until they learned their craft. Frequently an

victim's side as well, and US and ARVN troops soon developed effective anti-ambush techniques; armored columns, for example, developed the 'herring-bone' maneuver in which as soon as a shot was fired, all vehicles swung obliquely across the track, facing in alternate directions, and immediately opened furious machine gun and canister shot fire into the surrounding jungle. Another, wasteful but effective, technique was simply to drive an armored vehicle down a track or road which was suspected of harboring an ambush and spray any likely spot with machine gun fire as it passed. A single vehicle was usually ignored by ambush parties, and travelling at speed up and down a road at irregular intervals, these 'Thunder Runs' were highly effective in discouraging ambush parties. Another technique was the 'Roadrunner' in which an armored infantry company would cruise the roads and trails, stopping to make brief attacks on any spot which looked likely to be hiding an ambush.

Left: A bamboo breathing tube protruding from a VC hideout is discovered during a search and destroy operation.

Below: The simple lifestyle of the VC guerrilla is well illustrated by this view of a typical makeshift hut.

Right: A 'tunnel rat' investigating an underground VC bunker edges forward with torch and sidearm at the ready.

over-anxious member would fire too early, alerting the victims in time for them to take evasive action or to open return fire; the man detailed to stop the first vehicle might miss his target. And in almost every case, although the fire from the ambush was fast and furious, most of it was unaimed and at random, allowing the victims time to take cover and begin shooting back.

Ambushes are, to some degree, self-educating for those who survive, and as a result the Viet Cong gradually improved their techniques until they were a constant threat to the government forces. Fortunately, as we have said, they never attained a proper level of planning and discipline, so that they were rarely as effective as they might have been. Moreover, the education occurs on the

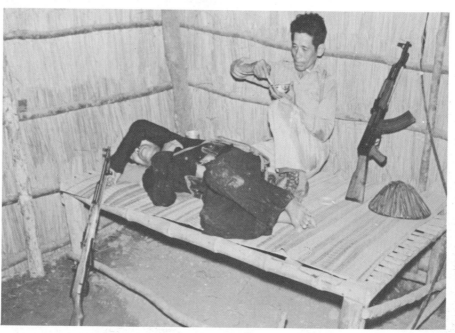

Once the ambush was over, whatever the result, the Viet Cong would melt into the jungle – unless they were trapped by American airmobile infantry dropped behind them, a frequent anti-ambush tactic. But once the guerillas were clear of the ambush position, they vanished into the local population. And it was this, probably more than anything else, which frustrated the US troops. The black-clad farmer driving an ox-plow, or carting a pig to market, or standing up to his knees in the water of a paddy field planting rice might be just a farmer, or he might equally well be a Viet Cong soldier; there was no way of telling, since both wore the same black 'pajamas' which were the universal Vietnamese peasant dress.

Left: This M48 tank of the 69th Armored
Regiment hit a mine at Cu Chi in 1966.

Below: Captured VC are loaded aboard a US
Army Huey.

Overleaf: The hut of a villager who has assisted the VC is burned by flamethrower. . Inset overleaf: A patrol of Montagnards moves through the hills. These highly effective irregular troops were trained and led by US Army Special Forces advisers.

Above: The commander of the Viet Cong's military wing was General Nguyen Chi Thanh – a general in North Vietnam's Army. Below: Viet Cong troops advance to attack enemy positions. This guerilla force depended upon aid from North Vietnam.

Pursuing an ambush party to a village brought little better results. Once into a village the fleeing soldiers simply vanished, either mingling with the genuine peasants or, in many cases, dropping into prepared hide-out tunnels. These tunnels were often most complex layouts which extended for yards in all directions, allowing men to drop in from one building, cross the village and surface in another building or even out in the concealment of the jungle. As well as acting as communication tunnels, they were used for storage of weapons and ammunition, food and other supplies for the guerilla groups, and could even be used as refuges in which guerillas lived for several days while searches were carried on above them.

It took the US and ARVN troops some time before the existence of these tunnel structures became known, after which it became routine to search every village for concealed entrances. Once these were found, the problem of clearing the tunnels came next; the immediate remedy was to drop a grenade or two down each entrance, but even after this it was necessary for somebody to go down the hole and physically crawl through the entire complex in order to certify that it was clear of occupants and to find what was concealed inside. This was an extremely hazardous task, since the guerilla in residence had all the advantages of familiarity with the tunnel and surprise, and some sordid and bloody hand-to-hand fights went on under many Vietnamese villages. US troops often resorted to flamethrowers in an endeavour to thoroughly flush the tunnels before putting a search party down, but this made their task even more gruesome and disagreeable. A technique used by the Australians in Korea was brought to Vietnam; they would pour flame-thrower fluid or gasoline down the tunnel entrances, thoroughly flooding the entire complex, and then, standing well back, fire a flare pistol into one of the holes. The subsequent ignition of the volatile liquid resembled a volcano in action and smoke and flame spewed out of every hole, frequently revealing entrances which had not previously been found; with this technique there was no need to put down a search party, since there was nothing of value left when the flames subsided.

In the closing stages of the war the guerilla activity became secondary to the major actions being fought by North Vietnamese Army units and by formations of massed guerilla parties acting as cohesive military formations, and the tactics of these units was in conformity with regular military practice – formal frontal attacks on well-defended positions and pitched battles in locations generally of the Viet Cong's choosing. But the guerilla activity never entirely died down, since it was the Viet Cong's way of ensuring that US and ARVN forces were spread thinly across the entire country instead of being concentrated against the NVA. So long as guerilla bands made sporadic raids and ambushes throughout South Vietnam, then the government was forced to disperse large numbers of troops to counter them, to make periodic sweeps, to search villages and catch what guerillas they could. Even if the guerillas never killed many soldiers in this phase, their nuisance value was worth several thousand troops to the Viet Cong because it reduced the threat to their regular formations in the war zones. Moreover, the propaganda value of the guerilla war was immense. Any attack by US or ARVN troops on a village harboring guerillas was automatically a 'massacre', and there was never any shortage of sympathetic press to whom the bodies of women and children could be displayed, even though in many cases the women had been active guerillas and the children had been carrying weapons and supplies for them. As noted previously, guerillas cannot win against a ruthless enemy; but when the enemy's lifestyle and society is such that ruthlessness is not permitted to him, the guerilla holds all the winning cards.

Top right: When North Vietnamese forces overran Quang Tri province during their spring offensive in 1972, they swiftly obtained these volunteers for the VC.

Above right: The war in Southeast Asia was not confined to Vietnam. Here Pathet Lao troops attack Thai positions.

Right: A typical scene along the Ho Chi Minh Trail during most of the war.

THE INFANTRYMAN'S WAR

At the end of the day all wars are won by infantrymen; strategic bombing, armored columns, naval blockades all have their uses, but victory is only secured when a man with a rifle stands on the ground he has wrested from the enemy. Or, as an American general once put it, "You have to have somebody to drag the other bastard out of his foxhole and make him sign the peace treaty". Infantry bore the brunt of the fighting in Vietnam and infantry, albeit North Vietnamese infantry, was the eventual winning force.

As with every other aspect of the Vietnamese war, the infantryman's battle differed considerably from the conventional war which American and other Western troops have been trained to fight, and in many cases their first task had to be to 'un-learn' what had been carefully taught them, and then set about learning a whole new set of rules which governed fighting in the special conditions of Vietnam.

There was, for example, no permanent, fixed, linear "front line"; no neatly-drawn strip of defences beyond which was enemy country and behind which was safe territory. Therefore there was no simple routine of a tour of duty in the line followed by a rest period in a quiet area. There were few, if any, quiet areas in Vietnam, and no military unit could ever sit back secure in the knowledge that it was unlikely to become a target for some form of attack. So that so long as a military unit was in Vietnam it could regard itself as 'in the front line' and the opportunity for rest periods totally free from threat never occurred.

The second major difference was that if the enemy were not in a specific area, neither were they immediately recognisable. To the occidental, all orientals look much the same; the average American (or Australian or British or German or any any other nationality) soldier cannot distinguish between North and South Vietnamese, Japanese, Burmese, Chinese, Koreans or most other Eastern races. The same problem might confront him in Europe, between, say, Poles, Czechs, Finns, Russians, and Germans, but at least there they would be wearing distinctive uniforms, driving distinctive vehicles, carrying distinctive weapons. In Vietnam the uniform of the enemy was nondescript, when it existed at all, and since the enemy mingled with the civil population and wore civilian clothing for most of the time, the Western infantryman might be excused for feeling that he was at a disadvantge.

Next came the terrain. Vietnam holds a mixture which ranges from mountains to jungle to rice paddy to swamp, and none of this resembles the habitual training areas of the Western soldier. Tactics, maneuvers and methods which work perfectly well on the heathland of Western Germany or the deserts of Texas need to be considerably modified before they can be made to work in jungle or flooded rice fields. Moreover the terrain concealed numerous hazards – leeches, mosquitoes, snakes, diseases of various sorts and of various degrees of risk – to which the soldier was unaccustomed and of which he had to be warned.

Because of these and other problems, the conduct of the war against the Viet Cong and North Vietnamese army took

Overleaf: A Jeep-mounted recoilless rifle goes into action against VC positions.

Below: South Vietnamese troops of the ARVN's 21st Division pictured during a search and destroy operation against the Viet Cong in February 1963.

on a special pattern. The Viet Cong operated not as a massed enemy on a defined front line but as a number of small groups, spread throughout the country, some of which would combine from time to time in order to carry out some specific attack or operation and then disperse once it was over. Accordingly, American operations were split up into frequent, concurrent, small-unit operations dispersed over the entire country as the enemy presented himself. Only by dispersing American effort in such a manner was it possible to maintain pressure on the enemy all the time; simply concentrating US and ARVN forces in one area, with the intention of clearing, say, one province and then moving on to the next would have had no effect whatever. The Viet Cong would simply have maintained sufficient activity in that province to keep the US/ARVN force occupied, while concen-

Left: A unit of South Vietnam's local militia is instructed in marksmanship.

Below: Two privates of the US 173rd Airborne Brigade, armed with an M16 rifle and M79 40mm grenade launcher man their foxhole at Bien Hoa air base.

trating their efforts into the provinces devoid of military effort. Dispersal, on the other hand, although flying in the face of the formal principles of war, was the only tactic which could place the widely scattered enemy forces under continuous threat.

The system was, therefore, to divide the country up into 'Areas of Operations' (AO) which were assigned to every ground unit, from the highest formation to the lowest; thus an army corps might have an entire province as its AO, while a platoon would have perhaps a couple of villages and their surrounding fields as their AO. Each AO had a ground force commander of appropriate rank, responsible for operations in the AO.

Although the AO was chosen upon largely geopolitical grounds – at the top level the AOs corresponded to the Vietnamese Military Areas – the disposition of units within them was governed by purely tactical and strategic considerations. This city had to be protected, that airfield protected, this road had to be secured against interruption, this area had to be controlled so that normal civil life could continue. Within the AO, therefore, units and subunits were spread about so as to conform with these various aims, and at the bottom of the ladder it came down to individual rifle companies setting up 'patrol bases' around villages, in the mountains, any location which permitted them to perform their allotted task and, at the same time, protect themselves from attack. Here they were on their own, at the end of a complex and tenuous supply line which ensured that rations, ammunition and other items were delivered with regularity, and relying upon radio communication to receive orders and pass information to higher formations.

Infantry operations in Vietnam can be divided into three types – dismounted – ie soldiers on foot; mechanized infantry – ie soldiers carried in armored personnel carriers (APCs) for greater protection and mobility; and airmobile, in which the troops were taken into action by helicopters, a method which gave speed, surprise and mobility to their operations. Broadly speaking these three systems, although they all existed side by side at the end of the war, came into being roughly in that order as the technical support became available.

Dismounted patrolling was some-times called 'a hot walk in the sun', and it sometimes turned out to be no more than that. But in most cases a foot patrol could expect sporadic sniping from the surrounding jungle and hills, if nothing worse. Ambushes were more likely than not, since they formed the Viet Cong's favorite method of fighting and were their most effective way of using small groups to inflict maximum damage.

The nature of the infantryman's war rapidly affected the type of equipment he carried. At the beginning of the Vietnam involvement, US troops used the same equipment that they were accustomed to using elsewhere in the world, notably the M14 rifle firing the 7.62mm NATO standard cartridge, but this was rapidly replaced by the M16 rifle, firing the 5.56mm (.223) cartridge, a change which gave the individual soldier a lighter and more handy weapon with lighter ammunition, allowing him either to carry more or carry something else. Unfortunately there were some technical hangups during the initial period of familiarization with the M16 rifle, notably the famous 'no-clean' instruction. The M16 used an innovative method of gas operation in which some of the prop-

Left: US infantrymen move cautiously forward to search a village suspected of harboring Viet Cong guerillas.

Below: A US rifleman fords a small stream, while keeping a lookout for signs of a VC booby trap in the water.

Right: The ARVN infantryman often lacked the resolution and stamina of the US soldier.

ellant gas behind the bullet was piped back to blow the bolt open. The weapons were issued with the notification that it was unnecessary to be too particular about cleaning them, since they were immune to fouling from powder smoke. Experience showed this not to be true and there was a spate of complaints about the rifles failing to re-load in the middle of a fire-fight. Investigation showed that the fault lay in an unannounced change in the composition of the powder in the cartridges; the new composition produced fouling which, when it cooled, set rock-hard inside the rifle's mechanism and prevented it from being operated. Some slight changes were made in the rifle and cleaning kits were issued to the troops, after which the troubles disappeared, but it took some time for the M16 to receive the full confidence of the troops.

The frequency of ambushes, and the need to be able to deliver overwhelming return fire at short notice led to some other innovations in weaponry. The 40mm Grenade Launcher M79 proved to be a most effective anti-ambush weapon. It is a single-shot, break-open gun resembling a fat shotgun and fires an explosive grenade to about 400 yards. With one or two of these distributed through an infantry squad, grenades could be rapidly shot into ambush positions, where their lethal area made them highly effective. Another loading, de-

Above: The Remington Model 870 pump-action shotgun was a useful close-range weapon.

Below: The standard US rifle for much of the Southeast Asia conflict was the M16.

veloped specifically for ambush use, was a plastic canister filled with flechettes or buckshot; on firing, the plastic split open to distribute the small projectiles in a wide spread across the front, so covering a large area at short range. Unfortunately the M79 launcher required the attention of one man, and he could carry no other weapon except a pistol, so that if the action did not require the use of grenades, then he was a passenger. As a result the M203 launcher was developed, a short tube mounted under the barrel of a standard rifle. This allowed grenades to be fired when necessary, but also permitted the rifle to be used in the normal way in the fire-fight.

Another useful weapon for infantry patrols was the pump-action shotgun, principally the Remington Model 870. Provided with cartridges loaded with

Below: A patrol of the US 7th Cavalry Regiment questions peasants about VC movements through a Vietnamese interpreter.

buckshot or flechettes, these became extremely popular with patrols because of the high rate of fire and the devastating short-range effect.

When not patroling the infantryman was living in his patrol base or fire support base, and was responsible for the protection of the base. Fire support bases, which contained artillery capable of covering the local area, were particularly attractive targets, and, as noted elsewhere, infantry and artillery worked closely together for mutual protection and support in these bases. The infantry's task was to keep the enemy from reaching the guns and howitzers, while the artillery's task was firstly to provide fire support for activities in the area and secondly to join in the defense of the base when attacked. The defense of such bases, and of patrol bases, involved careful selection of individual weapon positions to give the most effective field of fire and to ensure that adjacent positions interlocked their fields of fire and so did

not leave any approach uncovered. Barbed wire was staked around the perimeter and backed up with mines and trip-flares which would give warning of any approach and also cause casualties among the attackers. The 'Claymore' mine was favored in this role since it is a directional device which could be carefully sited to cover specific areas. The Claymore is filled with 700 steel balls set in an explosive bed and is electrically fired either by a switch operated by an observer or by a trip-wire or other enemy-actuated device. On detonation, the explosive propels the steel balls outward in a 60° fan-shaped swathe which is lethal out to 50 meters.

Within this perimeter were the weapon pits for individual soldiers with rifles, grenade-launchers and shotguns, and behind them were pits for the crew-served weapons such as heavy machine guns, recoilless rifles and mortars. All weapons were carefully sited and had their target areas accurately delineated,

so that even in pitch darkness it would be possible for them to open fire on prearranged areas without danger of hitting their own troops. As with all jungle warfare, the night-time rule was simple: stay in your hole – anything above ground gets shot.

As the war progressed, so improvements in equipment made their appearance and lightened the infantryman's load. Night vision equipment was among the most important of these innovations. In the early days of the war, night operations were rarely performed and the common saying was that 'The Night belongs to Charlie'. (Charlie being the familiar name for the Viet Cong, derived from the phonetic alphabet 'Victor Charlie' for VC and shortened to simply 'Charlie'.) Some World War II infra-red 'sniperscopes' were resurrected and sent to Vietnam where, in spite of their limitations, they were considered of value in night defense actions. Developments in electronic and optical technology since World War II had, by this time, enabled new types of night vision device to be made, and these were soon in use. These 'Night Observation Devices' relied on the technique of image intensification: the scene is viewed through a powerful lens which gathers whatever small amount of light is there, even thought that light may be so dim as to be useless to the naked eye. The light and shade in the lens image is then analysed and electronically amplified, so that light parts become even more light, resulting in sufficient contrast to allow objects to be distinguished. The amplification is in the order of 50,000 times, and the result is an imge in the instrument eyepiece which allows the observer to pick out man in starlight at 500 yards range or more. The adoption of these instruments, and weapon sights using similar principles, soon removed the Viet Cong's advantage during the hours of darkness and resulted in less night attacks and a higher rate of casualties when such attacks took place.

Other example of advanced technology to assist the infantryman included short-range surveillance radars and seis-

mic detectors. The radars were relatively simple units which could detect movement; they did not have the visual screen commonly associated with radar, merely a set of earphones which the operator wore. When directed into an area the radar signal was, of course, reflected from every object in the area, but did not register with the receiver. If anything moved, however, this would cause a distortion of the returning radar echo (technically called the 'Doppler effect') and this was processed so as to give a distinctive tone in the earphones. The higher the speed of the object, the higher the tone, and a skilled operator soon learned to distinguish between the sounds made by animals, men, light trucks, tanks or simply branches blowing in the wind.

Seismic detectors were buried along tracks and roads where it was suspected that attackers might come. They were wired to a central console within the base and the detectors would pick up footfalls or vehicle movement and relay the sound to the operator. Again, a skilled man soon learned to translate the noises he heard into accurate assessments of what was happening on the distant trail. In many cases the area covered by the detectors would also be covered by prearranged artillery or mortar fire, so that as soon as noises indicative of an attacking party were heard the trail could be bombarded. Another trick frequently used was to site a Claymore mine covering the area of the detector; as soon as a noise was heard, the operator fired the Claymore mine to deal with whatever was making the noise.

Right: A member of a US Marine Corps patrol daubs himself with camouflage paint and spikes his helmet cover with grasses.

The employment of mechanized infantry began with the US Military Advisers to the South Vietnamese Army in 1962. They were confronted with the problem of tactical movement in the Mekong Delta, an area of swamps and watercourses which hindered movement on foot, and it occurred to some of the advisers that the American M113 armored personnel carrier (APC) might be an effective answer, since these vehicles had a limited amphibious capability, enough to permit them to cross flooded areas and swim across watercourses. After some debate, two 'mechanical rifle companies' of South Vietnamese infantry were organized; each was divided into three rifle platoons, each with three APCs; a support platoon with four APCs, three 60mm mortars and three 3.5-inch rocket launchers ('Super-Bazookas'); and a headquarters section with two APCs. Each APC was equipped with a .50 caliber Browning machine gun, and 18 .30 Browning automatic rifles were distributed through the company for use as light machine guns.

While the intention was praiseworthy, the fact remains that the execution was initially poor. The ARVN soldiers were not particularly well trained to begin with, even in basic infantry tasks, and they had no conception of armored operations and no combat experience. The higher command echelons of ARVN knew little or nothing about the capabilities of APCs and therefore some of the

Top left: A casualty of street fighting is unceremoniously bundled into a groundsheet. Fierce house-to-house fighting took place in Saigon and the ancient Vietnamese capital of Hue during the VC's Tet offensive in January/February 1968.

Top right: An infantry patrol's radioman moves through shoulder-high vegetation.

Above: A US Marine patrol's light machine gun goes into action against the VC.

Right: An M48 medium tank attempts a river crossing.

first operations by the mechanical companies were not operations calculated to bring out the advantages of mechanized work. But the American advisers persevered, the soldiers themselves began to gain experience and take an interest in what they were trying to do, and after a shaky start they began to do very well. In three and a half months of operation during the summer of 1962 they killed 502 Viet Cong, took 184 prisoners, and lost only four dead and nine wounded.

The basic argument among those who support the use of APCs on the battlefield (and this applies today as much as it did in 1962, and to every army) is the question of what the APC is supposed to be: is it a 'battle taxi' which takes the soldiers in speed and comfort to battle and there ejects them to fight on foot in the traditional manner? Or is it an 'Infantry Fighting Vehicle' from which the infantry fire weapons and which maneuvers so as to take advantage of its mobility, protection and firepower to overcome the enemy? There are arguments for both sides, and today it is possible to see the results of that argument in hardware, as various countries produce infantry vehicles to conform with their own idea of what the answer

may be. But in 1962 this argument was in its infancy, for only a few armies had sufficient APCs to be able to conduct experiments, and even fewer had any practical experience of APCs in combat. As a result, the argument cropped up in the early days of the mechanical rifle companies, and in at least one incident could well have led to disaster.

In September 1962 the Vietnamese 7th Division carried out a clearing operation in the Plain of Reeds and, against the advice of the American adviser, one of the mechanical rifle companies was included in the deployment. It duly moved out, skirted the first objective, crossed a canal, saw a group of Viet Cong and promptly charged towards them. More VC soldiers appeared from the bush, and the nine APCs were rapidly surrounded by men firing rifles and machine guns. The ARVN soldiers replied, firing from the hatches in the APCs and firing the .50 machine guns from the roof. The action was now something of a melee, some VC attacking the APCs, others attempting to evade them; the ARVN company had made a fundamental mistake in charging straight at the VC instead of trying to outflank them, and the enemy were therefore

scattering instead of being concentrated.

The next error came from the American adviser who persuaded the ARVN company commander to stop the APCs, dismount the troops, and let them fight on foot; this was in full accord with the current US Army doctrine on the use of mechanized infantry, but it was doctrine which had been worked out for a Western scenario. What it did not take into account was that when the troops jumped from their APCs they were immediately up to their knees or higher in mud and water. So long as the ARVN had been in moving APCs, protected by armor, the Viet Cong could not get any effective fire to bear against them; but once out of the vehicles and immobilized in the mud they were an easy target, and indeed, it was this action which produced most of the casualties referred to above. After some indecision, the ARVN remounted their APCs and began to move, whereupon more Viet Cong opened fire from concealed positions in the swamp. By maneuvering the APCs to flush these men out, the ARVN company was eventually able to gain control of the area, and their net gain was 138 VC dead, 38 prisoners, and 27 weapons captured.

Below: An M113 armored personnel carrier of the US Army's 5th Mechanized Infantry Regiment moves across a jungle clearing north of Cu Chi in 1966. Note the 50 caliber heavy machine gun and its armored shield.

Although this operation ended successfully, it could have been more successful in that instead of scattering the VC, the APCs could have rounded them up. The most obvious defect, though, was that the American tactic of dismounted engagement was not suited to this sort of warfare, and from then on it became the standard practise to fight from the APCs, turning them into 'fighting vehicles' not 'battle taxis'.

Nevertheless, the success of the two companies led to the establishment of more mechanized formations. A number of M114 reconnaissance vehicles and additional M113 APCs were acquired from the USA and used to outfit these new units. The M114 was a light vehicle which had been developed by the US Army as an armored vehicle midway between the expensive light tank and the unprotected jeep. It carried a .50 Browning machine gun on an exposed roof mount and also an M60 machine gun firing from a pintle mount at the rear hatch, and it was somewhat smaller and more nimble than the M113. Unfortunately experience showed that it was a failure; it had poor traction in mud and had particular difficulty extracting itself from rivers or climbing steep grades, all

Above: A mortar team of the 101st Airborne Division lays down fire during operations in the A Shau Valley in August 1968.

of which were attributes undesirable in a scouting and reconnaissance vehicle destined for use in the Mekong Delta.

Another change which took place at this time was in the armament of the support company; the 60mm mortar and 3.5-inch rocket launcher had been shown to have insufficient range for the tasks they were asked to perform, and they were both replaced; the 81mm company mortar replaced the 60mm mortar, and the 57mm recoilless rifle replaced the 3.5-inch rocket launcher. At the same time the 'mechanical rifle company' changed its name to 'Mechanized Rifle Squadron'.

Confronted by these armored infantry units, the Viet Cong were caught at a distinct disadvantage, since their only weapons were rifles and machine guns, neither of which had much effect against APCs. Consequently when APC units appeared, the VC scattered. But they were soon hard at work evaluating the threat and calculating methods of defeating it. The first methods were rather crude; pits dug in tracks and camouflaged, so that an APC would fall in; mines laid at points which offered good approach to canals for crossing; the pre-

paration of dug-in positions so that VC riflemen and machine gunners could hide as the APCs went over them. And by the middle of 1963 the VC had obtained supplies of 57mm recoilless rifles, Chinese copies of the American weapons which had been supplied to the Nationalists in 1946. This had a useful shaped charge shell which was capable of making a hole in the aluminum armor of the M113, though their internal effect was usually slight and rarely caused the immobilization of the APC. Armor-piercing machine gun ammunition was acquired, as were anti-tank grenades of Soviet origin. By late 1963 the VC were using the 75mm recoilless rifle, another Chinese copy, which had a more formidable shaped charge shell and which was capable of doing quite serious damage to M113s. Finally the Soviet RPG-2 rocket-propelled anti-tank grenade appeared, basically an improved copy of the German wartime 'Panzerfaust', and the RPG-7, one of the most effective one-man anti-tank weapons ever devised. The RPG-7 and the mine eventually proved to be the most effective VC threat against APCs, and throughout the subsequent course of the war no satisfac-

tory protection from either of these weapons was ever discovered.

In 1966 the first US mechanized infantry units arrived in Vietnam. They had been carefully briefed before their departure as to the experiences of ARVN mechanized infantry units and, to their credit, they took heed and made preparations. They attended particularly to fitting additional machine guns to the tops of their M113s, surrounding them with armor-plate shields, since ARVN experience showed that unshielded gunners were favorite targets of VC snipers. In this way it was possible to mount a .50 machine gun over the forward hatch, covering the front of the vehicle, and two M60 machine guns alongside the rear hatches, facing outwards on each side. The Americans also changed their tactic to fighting from the vehicle; in this way they were to discover that they could avoid booby traps and mines set for foot troops, move rapidly through brush and jungle, and use the element of shock and surprise by charging VC positions with all guns blazing, only dismounting to secure the capture site. Another interesting technique they discovered, almost by accident, was that charging an APC across a flooded paddy field frequently flushed out VC soldiers who were lying under water, breathing through reeds, hoping to evade discovery and remain concealed until the US troops had passed through the area. But the prospect of being crunched into the mud by an APC track was too much for them, and they leapt from the water as the vehicles approached.

In 1968 the whole strategy of the war in Vietnam changed. For the North Vietnamese Army it was a change necessitated by their severe losses in combat and the gradual destruction of their clandestine organization throughout

Right: Infantrymen deploy from a Bell UH-1 Huey. Note that the helicopter's doors have been removed to speed-up their exit.

Below: A UH-1 Huey's crew chief mans the helicopter's pintle-mounted M60 machine gun as it leaves a landing zone.

South Vietnam. With their ground forces denuded of local support, short of men and equipment, and with supply lines disrupted, it became necessary for them to fall back into sanctuary areas to re-group. For the US and South Vietnamese forces their success meant that they could now devote their efforts to pursuing the enemy into these sanctuary areas and contain him there with constant pressure so as to prevent his return.

Illustrative of the type of warfare which then ensued is the experience of

1st Brigade, 5th Infantry Division (Mechanized), which had arrived in Vietnam by August 1968; it was, in fact, the last major unit to be sent to the country. It was immediately despatched to the I Corps area, south of the Demilitarized Zone south of the North Vietnam border. This was fairly open country and the M113s were able to move rapidly, to surround suspect villages and clear them, then move on again to make a second raid on another village. This fairly quickly removed the 'living-in' Viet

Cong and North Vietnamese forces from the area, but once the mechanized infantry units settled down for the night, their vehicles were easily visible – particularly in moonlight – and small parties of enemy would filter back, avoiding the vehicles and their crews. 1st Brigade therefore worked out an ingenious tactic to counter this infiltration.

Towards dusk, while they were still visible to VC observers, M113s would begin reconnaissance patrols. These patrols would continue into the darkness and, as the APCs were driving home, four-man ambush parties would be dropped off at pre-arranged spots. Since it was now dark, and since the vehicles did not stop, there was no indication to any watcher that anything untoward had occurred. The APCs would then take up their night positions.

The ambush parties were located fairly close together, so that there was no likelihood of VC infiltrators passing undetected between them. On the face of it a four-man ambush party would seem to be tempting fate, since they had few weapons and little ammunition, but they were little more than human trip-wires and were not intended to fight prolonged battles. As soon as an infiltrating party was spotted by an ambush squad, they would open fire, and as soon as the first shots rang out the nearest M113 would start up and, with headlights blazing, charge towards the ambush position, to open fire as soon as it detected the infiltrators. Once this technique was perfected it never took longer than four minutes from the first shot to dispose of the enemy party.

The third and most innovative system of deploying infantry to be used in Vietnam was by helicopter, the variously-called 'airmobile', 'air cavalry' or 'aero-rifle' system. The terminology is confusing, but by any name these were dismounted infantry – ie without armored vehicles – transported in helicopters; infantry battalions in US cavalry divisions retained the old cavalry terms 'troop'

Top left: Men of the US Army's 14th Infantry Regiment patrol through a rubber plantation, covered by M48 tanks.

Left: An infantryman prepares to set a trip flare outside the perimeter of his company's night defensive position.

Above: A class of South Vietnamese Marines receive instruction on the use of the M29 81mm mortar from their officer.

and 'squadron' for the sake of tradition, but underneath that they were actually platoons, companies and battalions like any other infantry. So far as employment went there was likewise little difference, except that 'air cavalry' units of the cavalry divisions tended to be employed more on scouting and reconnaissance tasks, replacing the 'light cavalry' patrols of an earlier age.

The helicopter was in its infancy during World War II and saw very little use. It began to reveal its potential in the Korean War, principally as a means of evacuating front line casualties very quickly and so enhancing their chance of recovery. After the Korean War the US Army began studying the application of helicopters to various military roles, particularly as cavalry scouts and later as weapon carriers. By 1950 an experimental 'Aerial Reconnaisance and Security Troop' had been put together and tried, and was recommended to be incorporated into divisional cavalry squadrons. By 1964 this incorporation

had been completed, every division's cavalry having its air cavalry troop.

During this period the Airmobility Requirement Board or 'Howze Board', under the guidance of Lieut-Gen Hamilton H. Howze and with the assistance of Lieut-Gen James M. Gavin, thoroughly examined every conceivable application of helicopters and reached the conclusion that helicopters needed to be organic components of almost every type of fighting force of the future; they visualized airborne infantry assault teams, the transport of artillery by helicopters, aerial supply lines, and recommended the establishment of a complete airmobile division. The report of the Howze Board led to the establishment of the 11th Air Assault Division, later re-christened the 1st Cavalry Division (Airmobile).

The airmobile division was originally seen as a formation for use in conventional 'western' warfare, and it was equipped with 428 Chinook and Huey helicopters. The Chinooks were basically the 'lifters', transporting artillery and infantry, while the Hueys were reconnaissance machines and were also armed with 2.75 inch rockets in order to give them a fire support capability. The

helicopters gave this division a flexibility and response speed which was unparalleled, and while this was welcome enough in 'western' warfare, it proved to be even more valuable in the conditions prevailing in Vietnam. Here the lines of communication were few and poor, the road network being sparse and under constant threat from ambush. Had road transport been employed in the traditional manner it would have taken many hours to move divisional units from base to point of contact, and their progress would have been impeded by factors varying from poor road surfaces to active intervention by Viet Cong. Moreover their line of march would soon have been signalled to the Viet Cong by sympathisers and agents, so that by the time the unit arrived at its destination the enemy would have evaporated.

Air mobility changed this dramatically; airborne reconnaissance could move rapidly across large tracts of country, could shift rapidly from one area to another, gave no warning of its approach and followed no constrained route. It could detect Viet Cong activity and pass on as if nothing had been seen, call for airborne reinforcements, and reappear

Troops unload supplies from a CH-47 Chinook during the setting up of a hilltop fire-support base.

later, from a totally different direction, to guide in an assaulting party which had the advantage of surprise. Once the assault party had landed on the ground and begun its operation, air support brought in ammunition and removed casualties or prisoners, while the air cavalry provided a constant source of heavy firepower on call to the ground troops. When the operation was completed, the ground troops would fall back to a pre-arranged cleared area to be picked up by their helicopters, while the air cavalry circled the zone and acted as a rearguard, preventing interference with the withdrawal. This sort of basic maneuver was soon overlaid with refinements as more specialised types of support were brought in to counter Viet Cong responses. Helicopter gunships were slowly developed; in the early days these meant little more than mounting a pair of M60 machine guns in the doors of a normal cargo mchine, fired by crewmen, but fleeting 'targets of opportunity' demanded heavy firepower and soon there were helicopters dedicated to aerial support, carrying rockets on exterior mounts and with banks of machine guns in the cabin. Then came the adoption of the multi-barrel 'Vulcan' gun, first in 20mm caliber and later in 7.62mm caliber, provided rates of fire up to 3,000 rounds per minute to swamp an area with gunfire.

It might be noted that the more publicized gunships converted from transport aircraft – 'Puff the Magic Dragon', 'Spooky', 'Stinger' and others – were not employed as infantry support machines. Their task was the strategic one of interdicting North Vietnamese supply lines, using flares and night vision devices to detect truck convoys and then attacking them with a formidable mixture of weapons ranging from 7.62mm machine guns through 20mm multi-barrel cannon to 40mm guns and even 105mm howitzers mounted in such diverse aircraft as C-47 Skytrains, Fairchild C-119 Flying Boxcars and the Lockheed C-130 Hercules. On rare occasions they were drafted into ground support roles, usually when some fire support base was under sustained attack and a gunship was conveniently located within striking range, and in these affairs their intervention was extremely valuable. But in general they were too cumbersome to give assistance in small unit actions.

The first air cavalry unit, the 1st Squadron, 9th Cavalry (Air), arrived in Vietnam in September 1965 as an element of the 1st Cavalry Division (Airmobile) and with only a brief interval to allow the setting-up of a base, began performing reconnaissance missions in the An Khe area. In October the entire division was committed to a major offensive in the Pleiku province, in response to reports of an alarming increase in Viet Cong strength in that area of the central plateau, and 1st Squadron was deployed to fly observation and scouting missions in order to find evidence of enemy activity. On 1 November a scout helicopter spotted several North Vietnamese soldiers and alerted the aerorifle company,

who promptly put a platoon in the air. Shortly afterwards the scouts discovered about forty NVA troops and the aerorifle platoon was called straight to the scene, landed and began a brisk firefight. It was thought unusual for a small NVA party to stand and fight rather than drift away into the jungle, but the aerorifle platoon killed five and captured 19 before the remainder fled. The reason for this sudden show of resistance became apparent when the American troops, sweeping the area for stragglers, discovered a NVA hospital concealed in a gully. There was more brisk fighting before the hospital guards were overcome, and the entire hospital was taken into captivity and evacuated by helicopter.

This early engagement by 9th Cavalry set the tone for their future work, and in the words of one official report, 'they virtually wrote the book on air cavalry operations'. The daily routine followed a pattern which became well established; information would be received – from agents, friendly civilians or from an outpost – of some form of enemy activity. A helicopter observation party would be flown to the area, usually an OH-6A Cayuse helicopter carrying the observers and two AH-1G Huey Cobra gunships acting as protectors, a combination widely known as a 'Pink Team'. If the observers thought that there was something on the ground worth following up, the next move was usually a ground reconnaissance. An aerorifle platoon would be flown in by UH-1D 'Huey' helicopters and landed in a location which allowed them to move out and check on the air observer's sighting. At the same time a standby platoon was alerted and mounted their helicopters; they would be called in as back-up if anything developed which was beyond the capability of the initial platoon, or they would be on call from another 'Pink Team' if one was making a reconnaissance elsewhere. If the back-up platoon was committed on the first sighting, then there was obviously sufficient enemy strength to warrant more strength, and the responsibility then passed from the hands of the air cavalry company com-

Left: Viet Minh artillerymen open fire on a French position using a 75mm gun captured from the Japanese in 1945.

mander to brigade or divisional HQ, and infantry or armored forces would then be deployed. Once the major forces had arrived the air cavalry were generally withdrawn; they were too valuable to be used in a full-scale firefight.

In discussing aerial movement of infantry, it is not unreasonable to ask whether the most basic aerial infantry system of all – parachute landings – was used in Vietnam; and the answer is 'Yes – once'. During Operation 'Junction City', in February 1967, 2nd Bn 503rd Infantry of 173 Airborne Division parachuted into the area of Katum in War Zone C in order to sweep through the town of Katum and clear it of North Vietnamese troops. They were supported in this operation by A Battery, 3/319 Artillery, who also parachuted, complete with their howitzers, to provide supporting fire. But although this operation was successful, paratroop landings were never used again. The jungle is not the best objective for parachute troops; they tend to be scattered across a fair area of country, and collecting them together is always the first part of an operation. In open country this can be difficult; in jungle it is well-nigh impossible and can waste an immense amount of time before the operation can get under way. The perfection of the helicopter landing technique, which keeps all the landed troops together from the outset, made paratroop operations redundant in Vietnam.

The Viet Cong were never entirely capable of dealing with helicopter assaults, though they were well provided with heavy anti-aircraft machine guns and always ready to use them. But the helicopters were usually deployed away from the enemy concentration, so that it was uncommon for a machine to be shot down during the 'insertion' phase of an operation. Withdrawal was a different matter, however, and it was vital for gunships to fly protective circuits around a landing zone while the helicopters came in to remove troops, since the Viet Cong would take this opportunity to close in and open fire as the machines were landing or taking off.

A far more dangerous ruse was to make some deliberate gesture of defiance and then sit back in a likely area and await an airborne assault. The landing

Above: An ARVN M60 machine gun team tensely man their foxhole.

zone would be ringed with anti-aircraft weapons and if the US troops were foolish enough to attempt a landing in the area, they would inevitably lose large numbers of machines. This ruse rarely succeeded, however; the air cavalry reconnaissance always looked the area over carefully, and only if it was quite certain that no ambush had been prepared would it clear the area for landing. In any case of doubt a helicopter would 'insert' a scout platoon who would check the area on the ground. One ingenious attempt to outwit this routine was the Viet Cong's use of captured Claymore anti-personnel mines. They had a danger area some 50 meters in front of the mine, and the VC would strap them to the tops of trees around a clearing, hook them together electrically, and then send out a 'volunteer' to mime some military activity in the clearing as an air cavalry reconnaissance flight was passing. If the scout helicopter, or that of the back-up aerorifle platoon, attempted to land, the Claymore mines would be fired as it came level with the trees, doing sufficient damage to ground the helicopter and severely injure most of its occupants at the very least. This, again, rarely worked after the first time.

The infantryman's war in Vietnam was a good deal different to what most infantrymen had been trained for and expected. It alternated between boredom and furious action, though that is normal for infantrymen, but it was not the orderly disposition of a front line, there was not the constant knowledge that the flanks were protected by other infantrymen, that the enemy was in front and everything behind was 'safe'. The enemy existed all around, appeared as innocent-seeming civilians one moment and armed opponents the next; action meant either hurtling to the ground from a helicopter, riding in an armored box, or defending a tiny fire base against what appeared to be an inexhaustible enemy. The fluidity and mobility of modern war meant that units would be thrust miles in any direction at a moment's notice, And rarely was a unit in one place long enough to become thoroughly familiar with the ground. Nevertheless, the infantry mastered their new environment and developed new tactics and eventually had the measure of their enemy. Most experts agree that success against guerillas and irregulars can only be attained with a numerical superiority of about 15 to 1; the Americans could rarely muster more than a five-to-one superiority, and the results they achieved with this are a testimony to their ability.

AIR CAVALRY

Vietnam was without a doubt the helicopter's war, with the US Army depending on rotary-wing aircraft for troop transport, fire support, scouting, heavy lift for engineering and logistics tasks and medical evacuation of battlefield casualties. It was perhaps the concept of airmobility, whereby air cavalry units depended on the helicopter rather than the earthbound truck or armored personnel carrier as their principal means of transportation, which was the key doctrine. By no means all US Army units committed to Vietnam were air cavalry, but every major unit did have its own helicopter companies which could provide troop lift when it was called for. And as a result of the widespread commitment of the helicopter, there arose the need for integral fire support for the troop-carrying helicopters. At first this was simply provided by arming the troop-carriers, but later there evolved the specialized gunship helicopter – arguably the most important new weapon to be produced by the Southeast Asia conflict.

The US Army's aviation units began their involvement in the conflict in December 1961, when the former escort carrier USNS *Card* arrived in Saigon with the 32 Vertol H-21 Shawnees of the 8th and 57th Transportation Companies (Light Helicopter) and their flying and maintenance crews. Within the month they were in action, airlifting Vietnamese paratroopers into an attack on a suspected Viet Cong headquarters ten miles to the west of Saigon. Over the next year the build up of Army helicopter units continued and early in 1962 the first UH-1 'Hueys' arrived in the war zone with the 57th Medical Detachment (Helicopter Ambulance). Army fixed-wing units were also deployed, these comprising a company of U-1A Otter ten-passenger light utility transport aircraft and the first OV-1 Mohawk reconnaissance aircraft. US Marine Corps helicopters also arrived in April 1962, when the UH-34s of HMM-362 established themselves on the former Japanese World War II airfield at Soc Trang 85 miles southwest of Saigon.

These early helicopter deployments in support of the Army of the Republic of Vietnam (ARVN) made use of early, piston-engined troop transport helicopters. They were in many ways a far cry from the turbine-engined rotary-wing aircraft which were to be deployed later in the conflict. The Vertol H-21C Shawnee was a twin-rotor helicopter powered by a single 1,425hp Wright R-1820 radial engine. Its performance included a maximum speed of 130mph, initial rate of climb of 1,080ft per minute and a service ceiling of 9,450ft. In addition to its crew of two, the H-21C could carry twenty troops or an underslung load of 5000lb. There was no built-in armament, but for operations over South Vietnam door gunners armed with 7.62mm machine guns were carried.

The Marines' UH-34D deployed to Vietnam in operation Shufly were single rotor aircraft powered by an 1,525hp Wright R-1820 radial. Its slightly more powerful engine and lower weight, made the UH-34 more suitable for operations in high temperatures or at altitudes than the Army's CH-21. The UH-34D had a maximum speed of 130mph, initial rate

Overleaf: Hueys approach landing zone.
Below: An H-19 evacuates wounded French troops from Dien Bien Phu in 1953.

Right: M60 machine guns mounted on a UH-1B.

Below right: ARVNs flown to a landing zone by a US Army CH-21 helicopter.

of climb of 1570ft per minute and a service ceiling of 9500ft. Its cargo capacity, a 5000lb underslung load, was the same as the Shawnee's, but its troop load was only 12 (plus two crew). No armament was fitted to the helicopter, but the pilot and crew chief were issued with submachine guns.

Early attempts to arm the CH-21s were not really effective and in order to protect troop-carrying helicopters an Army unit equipped with armed UH-1 Hueys was deployed to Vietnam in mid-1962. The UH-1As were armed with two 0.30in-caliber machine guns and sixteen 2.75in rockets, which were found to be useful in laying down protective fire to clear a landing zone for the troop carriers. The work of this unit, initially designated the Utility Tactical Transport Helicopter Company and later the 68th Aviation Company, laid the groundwork for the later gunship helicopters. Between October 1962 and March 1963 the unit flew 1779 hours in the helicopter escort role, accounting for an estimated 246 Vietcong casualties for the loss of only one helicopter badly damaged by groundfire.

By September 1964 more than 400 US Army aircraft were deployed in Vietnam in support of the ARVN. These comprised 250 UH-1 Hueys, nine CH-37 Mojave heavy transport helicopters, 53 Cessna O-1 Bird Dog observation aircraft, six OV-1 Mohawk battlefield reconnaissance aircraft and 88 utility transport aircraft. Personnel strength comprised 788 officers and 2975 enlisted men. This force was sufficient to assign a US Army aviation company (or US Marine squadron) in support of each ARVN division.

Below: A Huey air ambulance is directed into its touchdown. The landing zone is marked by the colored smoke, which also indicates wind direction.

Above: UH-1B gunships lay down suppressive fire on VC positions near An Khe.

Above right: UH-1 ambulances could carry up to six wounded on litters.

The CH-37 Mojave was a large and rather cumbersome heavy transport helicopter, which was powered by two 1900hp Pratt & Whitney R-2800 radials driving a single five-bladed main rotor. Its maximum speed was 130mph, initial rate of climb 910ft per minute and its service ceiling 8700ft. Clamshell doors in the nose gave access to a 1325 cu ft cargo cabin, which could accommodate two jeeps or a 105mm howitzer. An underslung load of up to 10,000lb could be lifted and 23 passengers could be carried in addition to a crew of three. Although the Mojave provided a most useful heavy lift capability, it could not compete in performance with the tur-bine-powered CH-47 Chinook which rapidly superseded it.

The first US Army airmobile unit to be committed to Vietnam was the 173rd Airborne Brigade, which went into action in June 1965. In August the same year an advanced party of the 1st Cavalry Division (Air Mobile) arrived in Vietnam, to be followed by the rest of the division numbering 16,000 men, over 400 aircraft and 1600 vehicles. By late October it was ready for action, receiving its baptisms of fire in the Ia Drang Valley the following month.

The standard troop transport helicopter of the US Army was the Bell UH-1 Huey. In its UH-1B variant, the Huey was powered by a 960shp Lycoming T53-L-5, later superseded by the 1100shp T53-L-11. It had a maximum speed of 147mph, initial rate of climb of 2600ft per minute, service ceiling 16,900ft and a range of 260 miles. Its cabin could accommodate eight passengers or three casualties on stretchers. Various combinations of armament could be fitted including 0.30 caliber machine guns, 2.75in rocket pods, 40mm grenade launcher, 7.62mm M60 machine guns for door gunners and even a pod-mounted 20mm cannon. The UH-1C had an improved rotor and greater fuel capacity, while the D had a redesigned cabin which could hold 12 troops. The UH-1H was identical to the D, except that it had the more powerful 1400shp T53-L-13 turboshaft.

In the early war years troop-carrying UH-1 'Slicks' would be accompanied by armed UH-1 'Hogs', which would lay down suppressive fire around the landing zone (LZ) to discourage opposition. Landing was the trickiest part of the

CH-34s from USS Valley Forge fly Marines into a landing zone.

helicopter assault operation, because it was then that the 'Slicks' were at their most vulnerable. En route to the designated LZ the helicopters would fly at an altitude of 1500ft or more to reduce the risk of groundfire. However, it was always possible that the Vietcong had ambushed the LZ, even though it was generally reconnoitered by a scout helicopter before the Slicks arrived.

Various formations were flown by the assault helicopter companies, depending on the size of the LZ and the urgency of getting the maximum number of troops into action. The most widely used formations were the trail, with each helicopter following astern of another, which was used to land troops in a confined area, or the V formation which allowed a flight to land in the shortest possible time without the helicopters bunching together and interfering with each other. Escort Hogs preceded the main formation over the LZ, with additional armed helicopters on the flanks and to the rear, if sufficient were available. The routes followed into and out of the LZ were always varied if at all possible, so that the enemy could not anticipate the helicopters' flight paths. Time on the ground was kept to a minimum and two minutes was reckoned to be the average unloading time for a twelve helicopter formation.

In addition to its troop transport role, casualty evacuation was an important mission for the Huey in Vietnam. The UH-1D and UH-1H could carry six casualty litters in addition to its crew of two pilots, a crew chief and a medical attendant. Although assault transport helicopters could be used for this task, generally specialized helicopter ambulance units were involved. More than

100 UH-1 ambulances were in service in Vietnam by 1968 and between 1965 and 1969 a total of 372,947 casualties were evacuated by helicopter. If the casualty had to be lifted from a jungle area where no clearing was available for landing, the UH-1 could lower a hoist and winch the wounded man up into the helicopter. Alternatively an emergency clearing could be created using explosives and chain saws. There is no doubt that helicopter evacuation of casualties, by enabling wounded men to receive skilled medical attention in properly equipped hospitals soon after they were hit, made an enormous contribution to military medicine. Only 2.6 percent of casualties reaching hospitals died and of the survivors 83 percent were able to return to military duty.

The evolution of the specialized attack helicopter from the armed UH-1 Hueys was one of the most significant innovations of the war, producing for the first time a rotary-winged aircraft specifically designed for armed combat. The Bell AH-1G Huey Cobra combined the Lycoming T53-L-13 engine of the UH-1H (derated to 1100shp) and the rotor and transmission system of the UH-1C with an entirely new fuselage. This was a shark-like, low-drag structure which seated the pilot and gunner in tandem, with the latter in front. Maximum speed of the AH-1G was 219mph, initial rate of climb was 1580ft per minute and range was 387 miles. Armament comprised a single 7.62mm minigun six-barrel, rapid-fire machine gun mounted in an undernose turret. This was soon to be replaced by a twin-turret mounting, which could carry either two miniguns with 4000 rounds of ammunition each, or two 40mm grenade launchers with

300 rounds each, but more usually comprised one of each weapon. Stub wings could carry pod-mounted rockets, machine guns or cannon.

Huey Cobra tactics generally involved the attack helicopters working in pairs with a scout helicopter to find targets for them. When laying down suppressive fire over an LZ they would fire their rockets into any cover which could conceal an enemy, paying particular attention to the troop-carrying Hueys' approach and withdrawal routes. When working with a scout helicopter the Huey Cobras would generally orbit above it at 1500 to 2000ft ready to engage any target found by the low-flying scout and to react immediately with suppressive fire if it was fired on by the enemy.

The attack helicopter enjoyed several advantages when compared to a close air support aircraft. It was far more agile and was able to make use of natural cover at very low altitudes. The view from the cockpit was far better than that from any close air support fighter and so the attack helicopter pilot could identify friendly troops' positions accurately and direct his fire to within a few yards of them. This capability was important when the enemy resorted to 'hugging' tactics to avoid coming under attack from close air support aircraft or the dreaded B-52s. On the debit side the helicopter was more vulnerable to enemy fire than a CAS aircraft, although armored seats and body armor for the crews often ensured that they survived.

The standard light observation helicopter for much of the conflict was the Hughes OH-6A Cayuse, popularly dubbed the Loach. Powered by a 317shp Allison T63 turboshaft, the Loach had a maximum speed of 150mph, an initial climb rate of 1840ft per minute, a service ceiling of 15,800ft and a 380 mile range. The normal crew was two, but up to four

passengers could be carried in the rear of the cabin. The Loach's armament comprised an XM27 7.62mm minigun mounted on the port side of the fuselage, which had a rate of fire either 2000 or 4000 rounds per minute according to the rate selected by the pilot on his trigger switch. An alternative to the XM27 was an XM75 greneade launcher. Additional firepower could be provided by the helicopter crew chief manning an M60 machine gun firing through the rear starboard door aperture (the doors themselves were often removed to improve crew visibility and to make it easier to get out of a crashed OH-6). Scouting Loaches often operated at tree-top

Above right: Troops drop from a UH-1 Huey as it hovers over a jungle clearing.

Right: The Hughes OH-6A Loach was the most widely-used scout helicopter of the Vietnam war. On this example, the doors have been removed to help crew visibility.

Below: Men of the 101st Airborne Division relax while a UH-1 Huey undergoes its preflight inspection in the background.

Above: An AH-1G Huey Cobra gunship flies low over a Vietnamese village. It carries rocket pods beneath the stub wings.

Left: A troop-carrying UH-1 lifts off from its landing zone. Note the cavalry's crossed sabres emblem on its nose.

height and below in search of such signs of enemy activity as tracks, campsites and cooking fires. When working with AH-1Gs the combinations were known as 'Pink Teams'.

Early in the war helicopter scouting was undertaken by piston-engined Hiller UH-23 Ravens and Bell OH-13 Sioux, both veterans of the Korean War. The UH-23D Raven was powered by a 250hp Lycoming VO-450 piston engine and had a maximum speed of 95mph, initial

rate of climb of 1050ft per minute, a service ceiling of 13,200ft and range of just under 200 miles. It could carry a crew of three. The Bell OH-13S was powered by a 260hp Lycoming TVO-435 piston engine and had a maximum speed of 105mph, with a range of 210 miles. Three crew could be carried. Neither of these types was used so extensively or successfully as the Loach, which began to enter service in 1966 and gave vastly improved capability.

In 1969 the US Army began to take delivery of a new turbine-powered scout helicopter, the Bell OH-58 Kiowa, to supplement the Loach. The OH-58A was powered by a 317shp Allison T63 turboshaft and had a maximum speed of 138mph, initial rate of climb of 1780ft per minute, service ceiling of 19,000ft and range of 356 miles. The normal crew for observation missions was two members, but up to five could be carried if necessary. Armament comprised an XM27 7.62mm minigun mounted on the port side of the fuselage.

In addition to the troop lift helicopter, a requirement admirably met by the Bell UH-1 Huey, air mobility required a medium-lift cargo helicopter for ferrying equipment, ammunition and artillery. This logistics support requirement was fulfilled with conspicuous success by the Boeing-Vertol CH-47 Chinook.

Alternatively 15 litters could be fitted for the casualty evacuation role, with two medical attendants carried in addition to the flight crew. When used as a cargo transport, it was found that the Chinook almost always ran out of cabin space well before its maximum weight was reached and consequently cargoes were generally carried as an underslung load. The maximum loads permitted for the various Chinook variants ranged from the CH-47A's 10,114lb cabin paylod, with 16,000lb underslung, to the Ch-47C's 19,100lb cabin load and 22,700lb underslung. The defensive armamant normally consisted of a 7.62mm door-mounted machine gun.

More heavily armed Chinooks than the standard transport version were used on occasion in Vietnam. Chinook 'bombers' were ad hoc adaptations which were used to drop riot gas or napalm onto Vietcong bunker complexes. The delivery method was crude in the extreme, with barrels of gas or napalm being rolled our of the rear cargo ramp and fuzed by a static line once free of the helicopter. A load of two and a half tons of

Above: Men of the 1st ARVN Division board UH-1s for evacuation to base. Helicopter rescues of troops under fire were known as 'Dust Off' operations.

Left: ARVN troops unload supplies from a US Marine Corps CH-34 under enemy fire.

Below: USAF CH-53s of the 56th Special Operations Wing aboard USS Midway during the evacuation of Saigon, April 1975.

The CH-47 was a twin-engined, twin-rotor machine powered by the 3750shp Lycoming T55 turboshaft. Performance included a maximum speed of 180mph at 10,000ft, an initial rate of climb of 2880ft per minute, a service ceiling of 15,000ft and a range of 230 miles. A crew of three was carried and up to 33 troops could be accommodated in the cabin.

Below: A Grumman OV-1B undergoes
maintenance in its sandbagged revetment.
The pod under the fuselage houses side-
looking radar.

Above: An OV-1 Mohawk fires a salvo of unguided rockets. Most Mohawks carried no armament.

napalm could be lifted by a single Chinook. In 1966 the 1st Air Cavalry Division tested three heavily-armed Chinook gunships. These carried a nose-mounted 40mm grenade launcher, 20mm cannon and 2.75in rocket pods on the fuselage sides and 0.50 caliber machine guns which were fired by crewmembers from the cabin side windows and rear loading ramp. The 'Go-Go Bird' Chinooks performed effectively, but it was considered that these large gunships diverted too many valuable resources from the primary transport mission and so no further conversions were made.

The Chinook's greatest contribution to the war was in heavy logistics support. Chinooks were used to establish artillery fire support bases on numerous otherwise inaccessible hilltops, lifting the guns into position and thereafter keeping the bases supplied with ammunition.

Although little used in the assault helicopter role, as the smaller UH-1 carrying an infantry squad was found to be more flexible and less vulnerable, Chinooks were often used as personnel transports. The helicopters' lifting capability was also used to good effect in recovering crashed helicopters and fixed wing aircraft, more than 10,000 being recovered in this way.

More specialized heavy-lift duties were performed by the Sikorsky CH-54 Tarhe, a flying crane helicopter powered by two 4800shp Pratt & Whitney T73 turboshafts. Maximum speed at sea level was 126mph and range with maximum fuel 230 miles. The Tarhe carried a crew of three, one of whom faced rearward and controlled the helicopter when it was picking up or dropping off loads. The external payload was 20,760lb, which generally comprised outsized

loads or downed aircraft, but a detachable pod could be fitted to provide mobile field hospitals, command posts or maintenance workshops. One of the Tarhe's more unusual loads was a 10,000lb bomb used to create clearings for helicopter landing zones in dense jungle. More usually it carried heavy engineering equipment, such as bulldozers, mobile bridges, 155mm howitzers or 2½ ton trucks. The Tarhe was also used for the recovery of crashed aircraft, especially those too heavy for the Chinook to lift. On one occasion it retrieved a crashed C-123 Provider, which had to be broken down into three loads.

Army aviation was primarily a helicopter operating force, but a number of important missions were undertaken by fixed-wing aircraft types. In the early years of American involvement in Vietnam observation and reconnaissance was

carried out by Army O-1 Bird Dogs. A more sophisticated reconnaissance platform was the Grumman OV-1 Mohawk. This two-seat, twin-engined surveillance aircraft was powered by the 1100hp Lycoming T53, giving it a maximum speed of just over 300mph and a range of over 1000 miles. The Mohawk's reconnaissance sensors differed according to the version, the OV-1A being equipped for photo reconnaissance, the OV-1B for radar reconnaissance using a sideways-looking airborne radar, the OV-1C had a camera and infra-red sensors, while the OV-1D combined the equipment of all the earlier versions. Normally no armament was carried, but some of the early aircraft deployed to Vietnam carried underwing gun and rocket pods. Among the tasks carried out by the Mohawks in Vietnam were the provision of photographs of Vietcong dispositions and installations, photographing prospective areas of operation, visual sighting of Vietcong units and artillery observation and direction.

A number of fixed-wing utility transport aircraft provided the Army with personnel and light cargo air lift within the theater of war. The heaviest of the Army's transports, the twin-engined C-7 Caribou, was passed to USAF control in late 1966. Thenceforth the Army was limited to fixed-wing liaison and light utility transport aircraft, with the USAF controlling all tactical transport aircraft. The DHC U-1 Otter, powered by a 600hp Pratt & Whitney R-1340 radial engine was one of the largest of the fixed-wing aircraft remaining in the Army inventory. It was manned by a crew of two pilots and could carry ten passengers, six casualty litters or 3,000lb of cargo. It was a STOL (short take-off and landing) aircraft able to operate from short and roughly-surfaced airstrips. The U-6 Beaver, also manufactured by de Haviland Aircraft of Canada, was a smaller light transport which also had good STOL characteristics. Powered by a 450hp Pratt & Whitney R-985 radial, the

Left: Part of the armament of the CH-47 'Go-Go Bird' gunship included 2.75in rockets, 20mm cannon and a 0.50 caliber machine gun firing from a side window.

Right: Australian troops board a standard CH-47 Chinook medium transport helicopter.

Beaver could lift a pilot and five passengers, or 930lb of cargo, over a range of 455 miles.

Two commercial light passenger-carrying twins, the Beech Twin Bonanza and the same company's King Air, were adopted for Army use. The Twin Bonanza variant was designated U-8 Seminole. Powered by two 340hp Lycoming 1GSO-480 piston engines, the U-8 carried a pilot and five passengers. The King Air variant, the U-21 Ute, was a turboprop aircraft, powered by two 550shp PT6A engines and carrying two crew and ten passengers or 1600lb of cargo. Its cruising speed was 248mph, service ceiling 26,000ft and range was 960 miles. A specialized electronic reconnaissance version was produced as the RU-21. Sprouting an array of external aerials and packed with special avionics equipment, the RU-21 was used for signals intelligence over South Vietnam, listening out for Viet Cong/North Vietnamese Army signals traffic which could betray the positions of enemy forces.

After the US Army, the US Marine Corps was the largest operator of troop-carrying helicopters in Southeast Asia. The Marine ground forces operating in the northern provinces of South Viet-

nam were supported by their own helicopter units. The Marines with their primary role of amphibious assault followed an entirely different operational philosophy to the US Army's air mobile units. The Army elected to use the UH-1 Huey as its primary assault helicopter, carrying an infantry squad. The Marines concerned with putting the largest force ashore in the shortest time while operating from the limited flight deck space of an amphibious assault carrier, elected to adopt a much larger helicopter. Their standard troop transport was the twin-engined CH-46 Sea Knight.

The Sea Knight was powered by a pair of 1250shp General Electric T58 turboshafts, giving it a maximum speed of 166mph, an initial rate of climb of 1290ft per minute, a service ceiling of 12,800ft and range of 211 nautical miles. A crew of three was carried and normally 17 combat-equipped troops were carried. In the casualty evacuation role, 15 litters were fitted and two medical attendants carried in addition to the flight crew. Because of the Sea Knight's size, it had a very useful secondary cargo transport role. In overload condition over 6000lb could be carried in the cargo compartment and the maximum external load on the cargo hook was 10,000lb.

The first CH-46s arrived in South Vietnam in March 1966 to supplement and eventually replace the UH-34. The helicopters were fitted with armor protection for the engines and crew and a defensive armament of 0.5in machine guns was fitted in the cabin to be manned by the helicopter's crew chief and a gunner. Early experience in the combat theater showed that the CH-46A model was somewhat underpowered, for example it was unable to lift a 105mm howitzer unless the helicopter was stripped of much of its internal equipment. Consequently an improved model, the CH-46D with more powerful T58 engines, was brought into service. In the summer of 1967 a total of 107 CH-46s were operating in Southeast Asia, this being about half the available force. From their initial deployment in March 1966 until May the following year, CH-46s had flown over 32,000 hours and up until that time their safety record had been good. However, there then followed a series of unexplained accidents involving the Sea Knight, leading to those in Vietnam being restricted to flying emergency combat sorties when no other aircraft type was available for the task. A

major modification program was then put in hand to strengthen the aft pylon, where it was discovered rotor vibration had led to structural failure resulting in the series of crashes. In the meanwhile the venerable CH-34 was returned to combat to fill the gap. Thereafter the Sea Knight performed reliably and well. By July 1969 it had completed over 625,000 sorties in South Vietnam, had carried 1,330,000 troops and lifted nearly 100,000 tons of cargo. In the casualty evacuation role it had ferried more than 120,000 wounded or injured men to the safety of base hospitals.

The UH-1 served the Marine Corps as a battlefield airborne command post and observation helicopter rather than as a troop transport. Its UH-1E was similar to the Army's Huey, but was fitted with a more comprehensive array of radio equipment and magnesium parts of the Army's UH-1s were replaced with aluminum to reduce salt water corrosion problems. It was this aircraft that the Marines decided to arm to provide suppressive fire during assault operations by the heavier CH-46s. The UH-1E's armament normally comprised two forward-firing M60 machine guns on each side of

the fuselage and two or four 2.75in rocket pods. This gunship role soon became the UH-1E's most important mission. In the year from mid-1966 to mid-1967 two-thirds of the helicopter's missions were armed assault support sorties, with the originally envisioned observation tasks being assumed by such fixed-wing aircraft as the O-1 and OV-10.

A natural extension of the Marines' armed helicopter program was the adoption of the US Army's AH-1 Huey Cobra attack helicopter. The first Marine AH-1G-equipped unit to serve in Vietnam was VMO-2, which received its first Cobras in June 1969. Reports on the Marines' early operational experience with the new attack helicopter were very favorable and it was considered 'a far superior weapons platform' to the armed UH-1E. Nothwithstanding this early enthusiasm, the Marines were not entirely satisfied that the Army's AH-1G met their special requirements. As a result of their criticism of the AH-1G, a specialized version of the design, the AH-1J Sea

Below: One of the Chinook's most important contributions to the war in Vietnam was the resupply of hilltop fire support bases.

Above: A crewmember fires a 7.62mm Minigun from the rear ramp of an HH-53 rescue helicopter of the USAF.

Cobra, was developed for service with the Marine Corps.

The AH-1J's principal difference from the Army's G was the powerplant. The Sea Cobra was fitted with a twin-turbine 1530shp T-400, which gave it a maximum speed of 142 knots at 2000ft, an initial rate of climb of 1820ft per minute, a service ceiling of 10,000ft and a range of 257 nautical miles. Armament too differed from that of the Huey Cobra, as the nose turret carried a single 20mm 3-barrel cannon, with a rate of fire of 750 rounds per minute and an ammunition capacity of the same number of rounds. Rocket pods or 7.62mm minigun pods could be carried under the stub wings. In the spring of 1971 a four-aircraft Sea Cobra detachment carried out an operational evaluation of the helicopter in Vietnam. In the course of this deployment, the AH-1Js flew a total of 614 hours and fired 14,950 rounds of

7.62mm ammunition, 72,945 rounds of 20mm ammunition and 2,842 rockets. It was considered that the AH-1J provided 'a significantly greater effectiveness in fire power over the AH-1G' and the helicopter's ability to maintain flight on one engine at 2000ft was found to be especially valuable.

The Marine Corps no less than the Army needed a heavy lift helicopter for logistics support, artillery lift and the recovery of crashed helicopters. In the early war years this role was undertaken by the Sikorsky CH-37C, a single squadron lifting a total of 12.5 million pounds of cargo during its Vietnam deployment from 1965 to 1967. However, a more powerful turbine-engined heavy lift and assault aircraft, the Sikorsky CH-53A Sea Stallion took over this role in South Vietnam from January 1967 onwards. The CH-53A was powered by two 3695shp T64 turboshafts, which gave it a maximum speed of 166 knots at sea level, an initial rate of climb of just over 2000ft per minute and a mission endurance of nearly one and a half hours.

Operating as a flying crane, the CH-53A could lift an underslung load of over 12,000lb, making it possible for it to recover any crashed helicopter except another Sea Stallion. Its 30ft long cabin could accommodate such loads as a 1½ ton truck and trailer, a Hawk SAM battery or a 105mm howitzer. In the assault transport role it carried 38 troops and as an airborne ambulance 24 casualty litters. In order to facilitate cargo loading the CH-53A was fitted with an hydraulically-operated rear loading ramp, powered winches and roller conveyors. The normal flight crew was three and a cabin armament of two M60 machine guns was fitted.

The recovery of crashed helicopters proved to be the CH-53A's primary mission. In the first four months of the helicopter's deployment (January to May 1967), a four-aircraft detachment retrieved 103 crashed aircraft, 72 of them CH-34s. At the end of May the detachment was joined by the remainder of its parent squadron (HMH-463) and by mid-summer the unit was carrying a

daily cargo load of 100 tons and this total increased to 250 tons on days of heavy activity.

The US Navy operated a number of UH-1B Hueys in support of Operation Game Warden, the campaign against Viet Cong sampans and junks on the Mekong River. This waterway and especially the labyrinthine channels of the Mekong Delta were an important supply route for enemy forces in the southernmost provinces of South Vietnam. Consequently the river was continually reconnoitered by patrol craft and air cushion vehicles, which could call on the UH-1B 'Seawolves' for reconnaissance and fire support. The principal Seawolf unit was VAL-3, which flew from such floating bases as converted ships and barges moored in the Delta. Armament of the Hueys was typically 0.30 caliber

Left: A battle-damaged Chinook is recovered for repair by a CH-54 Tarhe flying crane. The parachute prevents the underslung load from 'weathercocking'.

Below: CH-21 Shawnees were the first US Army helicopters to serve in Vietnam.

fixed, forward-firing machine guns and 2.75in rocket pods, with door gunners providing additional firepower with M60 machine guns and hand-held 40mm grenade launchers. At peak strength VAL-3 operated over 20 Hueys, which were divided amongst seven detachments flying from ship and occasionally shore bases in the Delta.

The Vietnamese Air Force was, of course, an important helicopter operator in its own right. The 1st Helicopter Squadron of the VNAF was formed in March 1958 flying the piston-engined Sikorsky H-19 in the search and rescue and liaison roles. Two years later this unit was augmented with CH-34 helicopters, used primarily for assault transport. As US Marine medium-lift helicopter squadrons re-equipped with the Sea Knight from 1965 onwards, their elderly CH-34s were passed on to the Vietnamese. It was not until 1967 that more modern Bell UH-1 Huey assault transport helicopters became available. As the Vietnamization program increasingly took effect in the late 1960s greater numbers of Hueys became avail-

able to the VNAF together with a number of medium lift CH-47 Chinooks.

If the conflict in Southeast Asia established the helicopter as an indispensible battlefield transport and attack craft, then it also demonstrated the helicopter's vulnerability. Over 16,000 helicopters were lost in Vietnam to enemy fire or accident, although a large percentage of these were recovered for repair and return to service. During the US incursion into Cambodia in the spring of 1971, Operation Lam Son 719, a total of 107 helicopters was brought down. The heaviest casualties occurred amongst the slow troop-carrying Hueys when they were at their most vulnerable – approaching or leaving the landing zones. Yet even these high losses represented only one aircraft shot down in every 4000 sorties. This is an indication of the intensive helicopter operations of the period and shows how dependant US and allied ground forces had become on rotary-winged aircraft for their tactical mobility, logistics and fire support. The war in Vietnam marked the coming of age of the helicopter.

ARTILLERY
& ARMOR SUPPORT

The employment of artillery in Vietnam differed considerably from its use in more conventional forms of warfare. If we take, say, the standard 'Western European' scenario of warfare, we find a firmly delineated front line, held by infantry; here are artillery observers who direct the fire of the guns and howitzers to provide support for the infantry and armor formations forming the forward troops. The guns are deployed some distance behind the line, sufficiently far back to be outside the area of the front line short range weapons such as mortars, but far enough forward that their range gives them an ample area of command inside the enemy's lines. The problem of protecting the gun areas is a minor one and is generally within the capability of the artillery unit. Further back are ammunition supply points and the positions for major-caliber artillery which provides the support for the division or corps. The whole system is tied together very comprehensively by telephone wires to that information and orders can flow in any direction and as much or as little of the artillery network can be brought to bear on any particular target as may be required.

The situation in Vietnam, though, differed from this ideal in almost every particular. There was no constant front line behind which the artillery could be arrayed and no layered deployment of corps, division, brigade, regiment through which the artillery strength could be sub-divided. The enemy rarely presented himself in an organized force which would attract the fires of massed artillery. The infantry forces were scattered in small groups, each trying to control a specified area, and each of these forces had its own small artillery contingent, responsible to it and rarely to anyone else. The danger of attack was so great that the artillery and infantry lived in a symbiotic manner; the infantry depended upon the artillery for support, while the artillery depended upon the infantry for protection. Artillery units were so scattered that they spoke to each other by radio; cable communication never survived long enough to be of any

Overleaf: US artillerymen were quick to adapt to the novel conditions of a counter-insurgency war in Vietnam.

Left: The Viet Minh won the artillery battle for Dien Bien Phu in 1954.

value. And instead of a neatly specified zone of fire toward the front line and an area of responsibility behind the enemy line, each artillery unit had to be prepared to fire in any direction, wherever the enemy showed himself.

This situation, though, did not appear cut-and-dried from Day 1; it was one which gradually evolved as the nature of the Vietnam war impressed itself upon the formal artillery organization and forced it to change in order both to survive and to perform its supporting function adequately

American artillery involvement in Vietnam had begun in the early 1950s with the provision of American equipment to the French, who needed it in order to replace the worn-out World War II equipment which they were using up. With the equipment came the MAAGs (Military Assistance Advisory Groups) but they made no headway with the French military authorities. The French were quite convinced that nobody could teach them anything about military subjects; moreover it appeared that the MAAG officers were anxious to provide equipment to Vietnamese units so that they could play some part in de-

fending their own country, an idea anethema to the French colonial army. Not until 1954, when it became apparent that the French were losing ground to the Communists, did the French Army agree to American officers being attached to Vietnamese units. When the French finally left Vietnam, in 1956, the MAAGs were at last able to spread through the Vietnamese Army; or, as it now became, the South Vietnamese Army.

Even then their task was difficult. Field artillery two-man teams were assigned to each battalion of the divisional and corps artillery. The South Vietnamese artillery was, at that time, organized with one 4.2-inch mortar battalion and one 105mm howitzer battalion per division; each battalion had three batteries, either of nine mortars or four howitzers, though this was later changed to six and six and finally, in 1965, the 4.2-inch batteries were replaced by 105mm howitzer batteries. In addition each army corps had its own corps artillery, two or three battalions of 105mm or 155mm howitzers, which could be used to reinforce the artillery strengh at any particular point within

the corps. It can be seen that this system, inherited from the French, was essentially the formal 'western' arrangement. But the artillery advisers from MAAG found that they could make little impression; their task was 'advisory'; in other words they could suggest but they had no powers to seek compliance with their suggestions, and since the Vietnamese appeared to have a totally different attitude to life and military activity than did the Americans, it was rare that their views coincided and that the adviser's advice was taken.

Vietnamese artillery was largely ineffective due to two principal reasons; firstly the dearth of trained and experienced artillery officers and secondly because they viewed artillery as being solely a defensive weapon. The shortage of officers was simply because the French had made no attempt to train native officers until 1951 and did not produce any Vietnamese battery commanders until 1953; and the three years to the departure of the French was not sufficient for these officers to acquire the sort of experience which is necessary in that job.

The deployment of artillery as defen-

Two M107 175mm self-propelled guns stand in firing position in front of a field artillery command post at Cu Chi.

sive weapons was partly a legacy from the French and partly their own predilection. The French had never had sufficient troops to control the entire country and in consequence the road network, poor as it was, was vital to their operations. The Viet Minh therefore concentrated on disrupting communications by cutting the roads, and the French response was to set up strings of mutually supporting outposts along the roads, each with two artillery pieces. The Vietnamese inherited this system and approved of it; indeed they carried the defensive posture to extremes, frequently refusing to place guns in logical firing positions for fear that they would be captured.

Nevertheless, with steady application the American advisers began to make some headway and they were instrumental in perfecting a number of techniques which, though appearing primitive, made the artillery more effective. Hamlets were given pyrotechnic flares or rockets which they could fire off at night to call down artillery fire if they were being attacked, giving the artillery a somewhat more aggressive role. The technique of lifting guns and their crews

by helicopter was taught to the Vietnamese and was used by them in combat long before anyone else. And the beginnings of a complex system of clearance procedures had to be worked out, procedures which, though often frustrating to the gunners, were necessary to ensure that friendly forces, civilians, aircraft or helicopters were not in the target area or line of fire.

The first US artillery battalion arrived in May 1965; it was the 3rd Bn 319 Artillery (Airborne) forming part of the 173rd Airborne Brigade, and no sooner was it on Vietnamese soil than it was ordered out to support search and destroy missions in the Bien Hoa area. Early in June came a Viet Cong attack on Dong Xoai, and the 173rd became the first US Army unit in Vietnam to engage in offensive operations against the Viet Cong by giving supporting fire to South Vietnamese troops during their counter-attacks.

In July the artillery build-up began, with the arrival of 2nd Brigade 1st Infantry Division with their organic artillery, followed in September by 1st Cavalry Division (Airmobile) and its divisional artillery. The 1st Cavalry divisional artil-

lery was typical of those which followed; it consisted of three 105mm howitzer battalions with 39 helicopters. Later arrivals often had a fourth battalion of three 155mm howitzer batteries and one 8-inch howitzer battery in place of the aerial rocket battalion.

This organization in itself was a reversion to World War II practise in that it emphasized the role of the 105mm howitzer. In Europe the 105mm howitzer had been relegated to a secondary role, since NATO doctrines called for the use of the 155mm howitzer as the general support artillery weapon. But in the conditions which obtained in Vietnam the small shell weight of the 105mm howitzer was more than offset by its lightness, enabling it to be helicopter-lifted into positions which would otherwise be in-

Below: A battery of 155mm towed howitzers in their sandbagged emplacements, with ready-to-use ammunition rounds nearby.

Inset right: The gun crew of C Battery 8th Battalion, 6th Artillery Regiment prepare to fire their 155mm howitzer.

Right: When firing at night, one gun in the battery would often fire star shells to provide illumination for the others.

Left: Marines of the 2nd Battalion, 3rd Marine Regiment hitch a ride aboard a searchlight-equipped M48 medium tank.

Below: An M48 provides support for the 3rd Marine Division during operations in May 1966.

accessible, or giving it a high deployment speed.

The standard 105mm howitzer at the beginning was the M101A1, virtually the same as the M2 which had served throughout World War II. Reliable and with a high rate of fire, it was well-liked by the troops, since they were familiar with it from years of experience. But in 1966 a new model, the M102, began to appear. This was a totally new design, but it was received with disfavor by the troops. It was low-set, which made it more difficult to load, had a new recoil system, had a small ground clearance and was more sensitive to bad terrain when being towed. In spite of this, though, it had many advantages, not the least of which was that it weighed a ton less than did the M101A1, which made it easier to manhandle, to tow and to airlift. A tactical advantage was that it had a small firing platform which permitted it to be swung through 360° very easily, allowing it to fire in any direction; the old model could only be traversed 23° right or left, after which it was necessary to manhandle the trail spades out of the ground and swing the howitzer bodily around to the new direction. Ballistically, the two weapons were almost identical; the M101 fired a 35lb shell to 12,325 yards, while the M102, with a longer barrel, fired the same shell to 12,575 yards.

A small number of self-propelled M108 105mm howitzers were also sent to Vietnam. These had been the divisional weapons in Europe until replaced by 155mm howitzers, and they were sent to Vietnam in the hope that they would be of use in mobile operations. But since it was too heavy to be helicopter-lifted, its use in such operations was restricted, and most spent their time in static locations, in the area support role, where their armored protection made them a useful 'pillbox'.

The next larger caliber to see extensive use was the 155mm howitzer, which came in two forms; the towed M114A1 or the self-propelled M109. Of the two the M114A1 was probably the more valuable in Vietnam, again due to its lightness which allowed it to be helicopter-lifted. The SP howitzer, admittedly the more modern and efficient weapon, saw less use, though it proved invaluable

in support of major ground operations, and it was also used as a direct support weapon for divisonal cavalry squadrons. Both the M114A1 and M109 fired the same 95lb shell to a maximum range of 16,000 yards.

The heaviest weapons in use were the 175mm gun M107 and the 8-inch howitzer M110; these were both self-propelled equipments which used the same tracked mounting, differing only in the barrel. Indeed, the barrels were readily interchangeable and it later became common for batteries to retain the same mountings but change barrels to suit whatever tactical role they were filling. The 175mm gun fired a 174lb shell to a range of 35,750 yards (just over 20 miles), while the 8-inch howitzer fired a 200lb shell to 18,375 yards. The M110

Top: A 105mm howitzer crew provides fire support for the 25th Infantry Division during operations near Pleiku in 1966.

Above: A rain-soaked mortar pit pictured during Operation Sioux City at the time of the 1967 monsoon.

was basically a World War II barrel on a modern self-propelled mounting; it was well-known and had the reputation of being the most accurate artillery piece in the American inventory. The 175mm gun, on the other hand, was a totally new weapon which entered service in 1963 and it went through a period of teething troubles before it settled down, taking some time to gain the confidence of the troops.

The aerial rocket artillery battalions were a new venture, being UH-1B or UH-1C ('Huey') helicopters armed with

Below: A formation of ARVN armored personnel carriers stream across the rice paddies during search and destroy operations.

Below left: The standard armored personnel
carrier of the Vietnam war was the M113,
which had a limited amphibious capability.
Below: This bridgelayer accompanied
armored forces during reconnaissance in
force operations to deal with water obstacles.

48 2.75-inch rockets. Under complete command of the artillery, and linked in to the normal artillery fire support channels, these machines acted as long range artillery, being sent out to bombard specific targets which guns or howitzers could not engage. In early 1968 the AH-IG (Huey Cobra) helicopter replaced the original Hueys; these were some 30 knots faster and could carry 76 rockets, and in 1970 the designation was changed to 'Aerial Field Artillery' (AFA) in recognition of their unique affiliation and role.

Transportation was provided, wherever possible, by helicopters. The airmobile division artillery was equipped with 105mm howitzers and these were lifted by CH-47A Chinook medium-lift helicopters. The Chinook can carry up to 33 fully-equipped combat troops, or an externally-slung load of 6-8000 pounds, depending upon atmospheric conditions. Eleven such machines could lift a 105mm howitzer battery complete with personnel and basic load of ammunition. 155mm howitzers could be lifted by the CH-54 Tarhe, which was capable of hoisting 18,000 pounds into the air, but where these were not available the howitzer could be quickly broken down into two loads, tube/recoil system and carriage, each of which could then be lifted by a Chinook.

The deployment of artillery in Vietnam was beset by problems, the principal one of which was the demand that the gun battalion had to be protected against guerilla attacks. This precluded the traditional siting of artillery well away from infantry locations, in staggered lines, and with fire direction center, mess-tent and vehicle lines distributed to the rear. Such a straggling position is ideally suited to European terrain, in which it can be blended and camouflaged, and to 'traditional' warfare. In Vietnam, though, such deployment was suicidal, since the artillerymen had neither the men nor weapons nor expertise to maintain a constant infantry-like posture of defense. What eventually evolved was the 'fire base', an integrated position in which artillery and infantry were mutually supporting. The location was selected by the infantry and artillery commanders working together, so that each could perform his allotted task; the artilleryman wanted a position such that he could reach out and fire at anything within his allotted area, while the infantryman wanted it central to his maneuver area and sited so as to give him a good defensive position. Fortunately these requirements were seldom conflicting.

Within the fire base the artillery arranged itself so that it could fire in all directions with minimum delay. Six-gun batteries were usually placed in star formation, five guns forming the points of the star and the sixth gun in the center. It should be appreciated that the pattern of shells falling on the targets reflects the disposition of the guns which fired them (unless special measures are employed to change this relationship) and therefore the star layout meant that the falling shells were well distributed around the target area. Furthermore, the layout meant that five guns could fire outwards from the base when under attack while the sixth, central gun fired illuminating shells to light up the area for the other five. Eight-inch and 175mm batteries, having only four guns, deployed in a diamond or square formation, with the fire direction center in the middle.

With the guns emplaced, the infantry then established their defensive perimeter as tightly as possible around the battery, digging trenches and bunkers, laying barbed wire, trip-flares and mines. Mortars would be dug in alongside the gun emplacements, and grenade launchers, machine guns and recoilless rifles spread around the perimeter. If light anti-aircraft weapons were available, particularly the M42 twin 40mm self-propelled equipment or the quadruple .50 machine gun trailer, these were sited so that they could perform their aerial gunnery but also depress their muzzles and act as direct support weapons. Their high rate of concentrated fire made them formidable and popular in this role, but since they were not to be found except in air defence battalions, they were not present in all fire bases.

The primary task of the field artillery was, of course, indirect fire in support of infantry operations within the maneuver area. But, when the fire base was attacked, as frequently occurred, then the firepower of the artillery was a decisive factor. The standard high explosive shell could be fired directly at the attackers, but better effects were to be had by employing special equipment or techni-

Below: 'Dusters' were tank chassis adapted to mount twin 40mm cannon and were especially useful in jungle fighting.

ques. In 1966 the need for a special anti-personnel projectile was answered by the issue of the MX546 'Beehive' shell. This contained 8000 flechettes, small steel finned darts about the size of a one-inch nail. The shell was fitted with a time fuze which burst open the shell in front of the target and liberated the darts, which flew forward with the shell's velocity. In spite of their small size they were extremely incapacitating; fired for the first time in November 1966 against a night attack, one shell killed nine enemy and stopped the attack immediately. It was later found to be useful in clearing undergrowth around a fire base to destroy cover, and also for flushing snipers out of trees and brush.

Another technique was called 'Killer Junior' and involved the firing of high explosive shells with time fuzes set to burst the shells about 30 feet off the ground at ranges out to 1000 yards. Gun

and howitzer crews were given cards which listed a series of range and fuze settings, and a number of shells with fuzes set were prepared every night, so that if the need arose defensive fire could be immediately brought to bear without waiting for the calculations to be performed. This system was considered to be more effective than Beehive, since the time fire shells drove their fragments straight down into the ground; a crawling enemy or one in a fold in the ground could escape Beehive, but not 'Killer Junior'.

An unusual problem faced the artillery commanders in the Mekong Delta. This area was largely river and swamp, and the dry land areas were usually occupied by a village or were so soft, due to the high water table, that after a few rounds the gun would break through the hard topsoil and subside into mud. Moreover the movement of artillery in

this area was virtually impossible by ground transportation and had to be almost entirely performed by helicopters. The question of firm firing bases was answered by the adoption of the 'airborne platform', a 22-feet square steel structure resembling a coffee-table, with four adjustable legs and large foot pads. This could be carried by a Chinook helicopter and lowered into any suitable position, whether it be river or swamp. The legs were adjusted to make the platform level, and the Chinook then returned carrying a 105mm howitzer, crew and ammunition, which it deposited on the platform. A number of such platforms could be placed adjacent to each other to provide a battery position. Whilst these platforms solved a difficult

problem, they had their disadvantages. The gun and its crew were unprotected, unless they were able to build a sandbag parapet around the platform, and ammunition had to be brought in frequently since there was insufficient room to maintain large stocks.

An alternative was to utilize the river rather than fight it. A 'Riverine Task Force' had been formed, an infantry brigade supported by a US Navy River Flotilla, and this had an artillery battalion allotted for support. At first this battalion shuttled up and down the river between a handful of fixed locations, selecting the one which could best support the Riverine Brigade's activities. But this was too confining, and in December 1966 the 1st Bn 7th Artillery

experimented with mounting its 105mm howitzers on a medium Landing Craft. It could then be sailed up and down the river to the best location and the howitzers fired straight off the vessel's deck. It was not entirely successful, since the craft was too narrow to permit the guns to be swung or the trails to be spread, but it suggested improvements. 3rd Bn 34th Artillery borrowed a pontoon barge from the Navy and tried fitting a howitzer on its deck, but abandoned this for a purpose-built structure concocted from a number of standard Navy pontoons fastened together and decked to make a barge unit 90 feet long and 28 feet wide. On top of this it was possible to place two 105mm howitzers, with a covered living space between them and protected

ammunition lockers at each end. Armor plate walls around the sides protected the gun crews when firing. The barge could be maneuvered by using landing craft as a tug or pusher, and additional landing craft acted as the fire direction center and ammunition resupply boat. Three barges and five landing craft allowed a complete battery to move at will in the Delta. The usual technique was for the barges to be pushed against

Right: A mortar round's time fuze is set by its crew. The setting varied according to range and whether an air burst was wanted.

Below: Armored personnel carriers add their fire in support of dismounted infantry during a fire fight with the VC.

Using armor in Vietnam was fraught with even more pitfalls and problems than was the use of artillery; indeed, for a very long time it was solemnly asserted that 'Vietnam is not tank country' and that was that. This belief stemmed from misunderstanding about the French use of armor and misapprehension over the climate and terrain in Vietnam. The French army had deployed about 450 tanks and armored cars, but, as with their artillery, they had too little equipment, too few troops and too much area to cover, with the result that the tanks were hived off in twos and threes and were rarely employed in operations calculated to give them the chance to function properly. There was also a great deal of misunderstanding caused by a widely published report on the destruction of a French mobile column, cut to pieces by a succession of ambushes. In

Left: An M48 tank of the 4th Cavalry Regiment advances, followed by men of the 14th Infantry Regiment in June 1966.

Below: Artillerymen prepare to reload their 155mm self-propelled howitzer during operations in the Mekong Delta.

the river bank in the selected area, firmly anchored, and then open fire. Accuracy was as good as with more conventional forms of emplacement, and the direct-fire capability of the howitzers also made the floating battery a useful clearer of ambushes as it sailed up and down the river.

The US Artillery left Vietnam with an immense fund of knowledge, most of it learned the hard way, which can be of incalculable worth if the counter-guerilla role ever occurs again. It is doubtful if anything of great value to 'traditional' warfare was learned, but what most participants agree is that the greatest lesson they learned was that of versatility. Artillerymen, as a class, tend towards conservatism; they take as their motto 'This is old, therefore it is good'. But their experiences in Vietnam confronted them with innumerable problems which no artillery had ever met before, and they rapidly dropped their conservative pose and proved themselves to be as inventive and ingenious as any other branch of the army in overcoming their difficulties.

fact this was not an armored unit at all and its fate had nothing whatever to do with armored tactics.

The climatic and terrain conditions in Vietnam were little known in the USA prior to American involvement; so far as the text-books were concerned, it was mountainous and had a monsoon climate. This was enough for most Americans; those who had served in the Pacific theater or in Korea knew what mountains and monsoons were, and assumed that Vietnam must have mountains with the same impenetrable characteristics as those of Korea, coated with jungle similar to that found on the Pacific islands, all well watered by summer rainfall which would make the country impassable for six months of the year. All this merely strengthened the belief that armored operations in Vietnam were impractical.

In fact the Vietnamese Army had inherited the tanks and armored cars which the French had left behind and were putting them to some use, largely in the same sort of defensive tactics which the French had employed. In 1956 US Army advisers arrived and be-gan to reorganize the Vietnamese Armor Corps along American lines, setting up armored cavalry regiments. Unfortunately all US advisers were bound by strict secrecy certificates upon their return to the USA after a tour of Vietnam duty, and they were therefore unable to communicate their experiences to the rest of the US Armored Force, with the result that the misconceptions about the employment of armor in Vietnam were never corrected.

Under the guidance of the US advisers the Vietnamese armored troops moved away from their basically defensive attitude and began to use their tanks in a more aggressive manner. The results varied; sometimes the armor would win a decisive victory, sometimes it would be poorly handled and fail. The basic fault appeared to be carelessness; gunnery was poor, the gunners relying more upon firing many shots in the enemy's general direction rather than upon fewer but better-aimed shots; tanks tended to bunch closely, presenting an enemy with several alternative targets in a small compass; and troops lost their aggressiveness and were content to make a stand, treat-ing the tanks as mobile pillboxes. On the whole, though, the results, when analysed by the higher echelons in the US Army, suggested that perhaps there was scope for more armor in the combat zone, and that perhaps US armored forces could, after all, be usefully employed there.

In early 1965 the American command in Vietnam had reached the conclusion that the South Vietnamese Army was no longer able to hold off the enemy's attacks and that US forces would be required to give assistance. The first result of this was a request for two Marine battalion landing teams to assist the ARVN in making the airfield at Da Nang secure. On 9th March 1965 the first US armor arrived when an M48A3 tank of the 3rd Platoon, Company B, 3rd Marine Tank Battalion rolled off a landing craft on to the beach at Da Nang. It was followed in a few days by another platoon, and later by the remainder of the battalion. Among their vehicles were a number of flame-thrower tanks which were found particularly effective in clearing ambushes. Marine Corps tanks took part in one of the first major battles involving US troops, Operation Starlite, a pre-emptive thrust designed to break up a Viet Cong attack on the Chu Lai airfield southeast of Da Nang. Three Marine battalions were used, each with a tank platoon in support, and the two-day operation was extremely successful, the Marines eventually trapping the Viet Cong with their backs to the sea and killing over 700.

Nevertheless, there was still great resistance in the US to the suggestion that armored forces should go to Vietnam. As late as July 1965 the US Chief of Staff, General Harold K. Johnson, expressed an opinion that tanks were likely to be of little use in Vietnam, though he approved of the 1st Infantry Division taking one squadron of tanks along as an experiment. In his reply, General Westmoreland, who was then Commanding US forces in Vietnam, said that 'except for a few coastal areas . . . Vietnam is no place for either tank or mechanized infantry units'.

Left: This mortar formed part of the perimeter defenses of Fire Base 14 near Kontum, manned by the 35th Inf. Regt.

Stripped of most of their tanks, the armored element of 1st Infantry Division re-equipped with modified M113 armored personnel carriers (APCs); these were rapidly fitted with shields and additional machine guns to act as a sort of light tank or reconnaissance vehicle. After arrival in Vietnam the M48A3 tanks which the divisional cavalry squadron had been permitted to keep, in accordance with General Johnson's directive, were taken from them and sequestered in a base depot, and it was to be six months before it was possible to get them out and put them to use.

With their strengthened M113s, now known as 'ACAVs' (Armored Cavalry Assault Vehicles) 1st Division began aggressive patrolling. Soon they were involved in a number of small actions which, though not of great strategic significance, nevertheless showed that the ACAVs were capable of adding tactical flexibility to even the simplest encounter. ACAVs in a defensive position acted as armored strongpoints, had heavy fire power from their .50 machine guns, and could be rapidly moved from

one threatened point of the perimeter to another to counter changing attack patterns. Accompanying patrols they had the ability to churn through flooded paddy fields and drainage canals, so cutting around ambushes which, hitherto, had relied upon waterways to keep the approaching patrols channeled into the danger area. Gradually it came to be acknowledged that armored vehicles could move easily in most of the Vietnam terrain and that there might be a role for them after all.

In April 1966 came what amounted to a breakthrough in the employment of armor. The 1st Cavalry Division were conducting an operation west of Plei Me and requested the support of 175mm guns and 8-inch howitzers, both self-propelled equipments. This involved moving the artillery through several miles of trackless jungle, and it was decided to build an armored column to escort the guns. 3rd Squadron, 4th Cavalry, with nine M48A3 tanks and 17 ACAVs formed an escort, and the tanks carved their way through the jungle to the chosen location, with the ACAVs

Above: Clips of 40mm ammunition are loaded into the cannon of these 'Dusters' of B Battery, 60th Artillery Regiment, 1967.

shepherding the artillery and their ammunition and supply train along behind. The move was successfully completed, and while the artillery fired its missions, for two days the tanks scoured the nearby hills and valleys for signs of the enemy. When the mission was completed the column formed up once more and went back to base. The tanks had notched up almost 100 miles of jungle operation without mishap, a performance which went a long way to convincing the doubters that armor had its place in Vietnam.

As armor began to earn its place in the order of battle, so the armored troops discovered that their views on tactics were going to have to change. The tactical maneuvers designed for use in Europe had no place in the confined spaces of dirt roads and jungle tracks, and the operations to counter guerilla warfare had no resemblance to those designed to counter a sophisticated armored enemy.

In the early days only the protection, mobility and firepower of the armor managed to save them from tactical blunders, but, as in all similar cases, those who survive learn quickly.

The basic military task was still, as it had been in French days, to command the road network and thus ensure that communications were preserved, and the principal Viet Cong maneuver, as with most types of irregular force, was the ambush. On the face of it the armored column should have been the answer to this, given that the vehicles were bullet-proof and carried ample retaliatory weapons, but once confronted with armor the Viet Cong were not slow to go to their Soviet masters and ask for anti-armor weapons. These came in the form of the notorious RPG-7 rocket launchers, one of the most effective one-man anti-tank weapons ever devised. Fired from the shoulder, the RPG-7 has a range of about 500 meters and is fitted with a shaped-charge warhead which can blast through 12 inches of armor plate. Equipped with these the Viet Cong were able to present a formidable threat to armored vehicles, and it became necessary to develop special tactics to defeat ambushes.

The system involved the alerting of artillery and airmobile infantry prior to any armored movement along a road where ambushes might reasonably be expected. Once the ambush was sprung the traditional roles of infantry and armor were reversed: the armor would hold the enemy in position, counterfiring at the ambush party, while the infantry were helicoptered in to flanking positions from which they could move

Left: USAF security police prepare to move out with an ARVN tank to clear VC forces from an air base's perimeter.

Below: Armor and infantry operate together during a reconnaissance in force mission against Viet Cong/North Vietnamese Army forces.

and cut into the rear of the ambush party. Artillery fire on pre-arranged locations effectively sealed off any escape routes, and it was simply a matter of squeezing the ambush between the infantry and the armor. In retaliation the Viet Cong turned to the use of mines to defeat the armored vehicle. These could be laid on any road or track which was likely to carry armor, and whilst the effect was not necessarily tied in with an ambush or with any other operation, the attrititon of vehicles due to mines was serious and reduced the amount of armor available for escorting duties along the roads. One mechanized infantry unit had 14 M113 APCs mined in eight days operations, and only eight of these vehicles were repairable. Tanks, due to their greater thickness of armor, suffered less from mines; they were frequently immobilized for a time, but the hull was rarely damaged and the crew and internal equipment was unhurt. But APCs and ACAVs with much thinner armor were at considerable risk; gasoline-fuelled APCs invariably burst into flames when mined, killing or severely wounding most of the crew. The driver was particularly vulnerable, seated alongside the engine, and it became cus-

tomary for crew members to rotate this task between them. Countering the mine took two forms; firstly to prevent the enemy laying them, and secondly to discover them before they were triggered by a vehicle. Analysis of mine casualties showed that they had a tendency to appear in the same locations, and these locations proved to have similar characteristics – proximity to Viet Cong areas, covered routes in and out, high frequency of armor movements. Once this pattern was recognized it became possible to forecast where mining activity would occur and place ambush parties in the vicinity or bury sensors which would alert patrols. Some units preferred a more direct method, simply driving a tank or ACAV at high speed down the suspect road at odd times during the night, spraying the likely areas with gunfire in the hope of catching a mining party at work.

Attempts to detect mines were sporadically successful; the principal difficulty was that the Viet Cong were not using a standard pattern of mine but would use any explosive device which could be made to function. These ranged from standard Soviet anti-tank mines to improvised boxes of explosives with sim-

ple trip-wire fuzes, to artillery shells and aerial bombs with pressure-sensitive fuzes. Some of these could be detected by the traditional methods of electro-acoustic detector or prodder, though this was a slow business. Others did not respond to this type of detector. Armored crew men made various attempts to reinforce their vehicles against mines, but these were often self-defeating. One unit laid sandbags inside their M113 APCs, covering the floor, so as to absorb the blast and fragments due to mine detonation; within six weeks they had fourteen vehicles broken down due to transmission failure from the excess weight.

In 1969 an Expendable Mine Roller was delivered for test in Vietnam. This was an M48 tank which pushed a multiple roller ahead of it, so that the mines would be triggered by the weight of the roller. It was a cumbersome device, and less than successful in soft ground, where the rollers frequently sank under their own weight (20 tons) and stalled the pusher tank. But it proved moderately successful in good terrain and eventually 27 were in use in Vietnam. They were not, however, the complete answer to the mine, and, indeed, the problem is still being studied.

Early in 1968 the North Vietnamese Army and the Viet Cong mounted their Tet offensive ('Tet' meaning the lunar New Year), and in the several battles which took place armored forces proved invaluable. In Hue, where the longest individual battle took place, ground cavalry, US Marine armor and South Vietnamese armor fought for 26 days in a densely populated area. Due to the close terrain, anti-tank weapons were used in profusion, and some tanks sustained as many as fifteen rocket strikes; though these did not impair the efficiency of the tanks they were so wearing on the occupants that crews had to be changed every 24 hours. With the direction of Viet Cong attacks varying from hour to hour, the mobility of the armored forces, which enabled them to move rapidly from one threatened area to another, was of inestimable value, and their firepower eventually wore out the attackers. In the Saigon area there were 79 separate engagements during the offensive and armor played a vital part in 37 of them.

The Tet offensive was followed by two more concerted Viet Cong efforts, the last of which was specifically directed against US troop concentrations and bases rather than against South Vietnamese installations or civil targets. This led to intense battles over a wide area, but, again, armored forces were invaluable in providing highly mobile striking forces which could maneuver rapidly and concentrate sufficient force to defeat every attack. In all the three offensives covered a period of seven months, but their defeat was such that they were the last concerted offensives to be mounted by the Viet Cong; they lost over 60,000 troops in battle, and the counter-strokes by US and South Vietnamese forces carried the battle back to the borders of South Vietnam and beyond.

Top right: A flame-throwing tank in action.

Above right: An M48 tank of an ARVN armored regiment in action in the Quang Tri area near the Demilitarized Zone.

Right: Infantry supported by armor carry out a house-to-house search for VC.

Below: 105mm howitzers positioned on a hilltop fire base. In many cases the guns were protected by sandbagged emplacements.

Inset: A 105mm howitzer of the 11th Artillery Regiment in action at Fire Support Base 'Charlie 2' near the DMZ.

THE NORTH VIETNAMESE ARMY

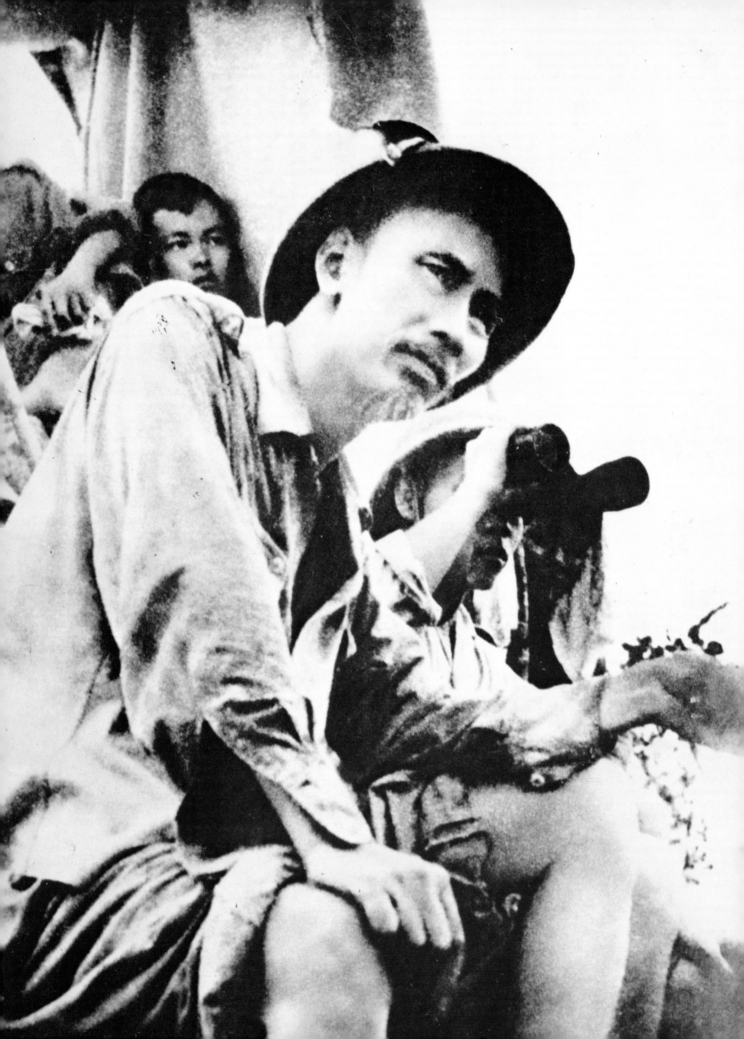

Remembering that the North Vietnamese Army was put together under the leadership of General Giap, who was trained by the Chinese Communists, it can be expected that the army was modelled upon Chinese and ultimately, Russian lines. And although both these countries make a great deal of play of such resounding phrases as the 'Marxist-Leninist Doctrine of Warfare' and the 'Revolutionary Theory of War', the fact remains that they are both sufficiently pragmatic to organize their forces along lines which have almost become hallowed by time. The organizational structure of the North Vietnamese Army is, therefore, the conventional pyramid, with a headquarters at the top and a graduated scale of armies, divisions, brigades, battalions and companies leading down to the platoons of soldiers which form the base.

Within that formal structure, though, there are considerable differences to Western armies which use similar forms. In its early days, the late 1950s, the NVA was, like all peasant revolutionary armies, weighted disproportionately to infantry. Revolutionary forces regard manpower as their prime currency and there is never any shortage of it in Far Eastern nations. Tasks which any Western army would require machinery to perform – road-building, bridging, carriage of stores and equipment – a Far Eastern peasant army simply swamps with men. It would obviously be illogical and uneconomic to retain vast pools of manpower for such tasks; therefore when not building roads or performing other laboring tasks, the manpower reverts to its primary function of infantry. Infantry are the easiest troops to train, provided their equipment is kept at a fairly low technological level and their tactics simple, and it is standard practise in any army to teach all recruits to be infantrymen before select-

ing those with various abilities for further training in specialized roles – artillerymen, tank crews, radar operators or whatever. So the infant North Vietnamese Army cast its conscriptive net widely and drew in a vast pool of men which it then proceeded to train in the basic infantry techniques.

It was helped in this by several tens of thousands of South Vietnamese soldiers whose political aspirations or preferences led them to move north in 1954 and become the cadre of the NVA. These men had been trained and were combat veterans of one degree or another, and their example and teachings soon brought the NVA to a basic level of competence.

The next question was how to equip this force; indeed, questions of equipment and training go hand in hand, for it

is necessary to decide upon the equipment before the training can begin. Here the Communist Party links with Russia and China paid dividends, both countries being willing to provide arms and ammunition on exceedingly favorable terms. In addition there was a considerable stock of weapons left behind by the French which could be used. These varying sources resulted in the NVA being outfitted with a heterogenous collection of weapons to begin with.

From the French there were Lebel bolt-action rifles and MAT-38 submachine guns, Chatellerault M1928 and Hotchkiss machine guns, some light artillery and a handful of ex-American M24 light tanks, and most of this stock was old, worn and reaching the end of its useful life. Nevertheless, it was satisfactory for training and was taken into use.

Overleaf: victorious Viet Minh troops cluster around a wrecked C-47 transport.

Left: Ho Chi Minh was the founder of the Viet Minh and leader of North Vietnam until his death in 1969.

Above right: Vietnamese junks were used to smuggle arms to Viet Cong forces.

Right: A Viet Minh artillery unit in action against the French during the mid-1950s.

From China and Russia came rather more modern equipment; PPSh and PPS-42 submachine guns, surplus to Soviet requirements; Simonov SKS automatic rifles, both in Soviet pattern and in the Chinese 'Type 56' copy pattern; Mosin-Nagant Model 1944 bolt-action carbines, again both in the Russian original form and as the Chinese 'Type 53' copy; Soviet Degtyarev 'DP' machine guns and Maxim machine guns; in other words all the weapons that both China and Russia had plenty of, had replaced in their own services by better weapons, and were happy to be rid of at a price. Moreover the Chinese also handed over quite substantial stocks of ex-American weapons – Garand M1 rifles, M1 carbines, M3 submachine guns – which had been originally supplied to the Chinese Nationalist Army and then acquired by the Chinese Communist when they took over the country in 1949.

These basic weapons were then augmented by heavier equipment. Soviet artillery pieces, notably the M1942 76mm divisional gun, which also had a Chinese equivalent, the Type 54, and the 122mm M1938 howitzer became the standard divisional artillery. Infantry heavy weapons companies were provided with Soviet 81mm and 120mm mortars, while the company headquarters was given one of two Soviet 14.5mm anti-tank rifles. China also off-loaded a collection of ex-Japanese artillery, 75mm and 105mm field guns and howitzers, and a number of the tiny 70mm Infantry Howitzer which, for all its frailty, was a useful weapon in jungle fighting.

Finally, there was a small number of tanks, the ageing T-34 which had performed so well in World War II and which had now been replaced by better models in the armies of the Warsaw Pact. Nevertheless it was still a valid weapon, reliable, with a moderately powerful 76mm gun and, above all, it was simple to operate and maintain, exactly what was required by the recruits of Giap's new army.

With this as his basis, Giap began building. There were two major objectives, firstly the strengthening of North Vietnam as an independent nation and the provision of an army to defend it; and

Above: Artillerymen of the North Vietnamese Army are instructed in the use of the infantry howitzer in the late 1950s.

secondly the liberation of South Vietnam and its incorporation into a unified state. The first required a nominal army, but the second required numbers. The first step was to train the South Vietnamese Communists in basic guerilla tactics and feed them back into the South to take up 'sleeping' positions until they were required to function. Once this was under way, training of the NVA increased and so did its numbers, as the recruitment base was widened and conscription bit into the peasantry. In addition to the army, which had a theoretical ceiling of about half a million men, there was also the 'People's Armed Security Force', the 'Frontier Security Force' and the 'Coastal Security Force', all of the usual type of armed para-military force necessary in Communist states to keep the victims inside, and a 'People's Armed Militia' which was a species of home guard force organized by regions. Altogether these para-military forces totalled some 450,000, which meant that Giap had a recruiting target of about one million men (and women; the Militia and guerilla forces incorporated women as well as men throughout their rank structure.)

The population of North Vietnam was about 22 million and the birthrate had always been such that in any year there was a near-certainty that there would be a surplus of able-bodied males above the army requirements; a two-year term of conscription was made mandatory, to be followed by a term of 'reserve' service during which the discharged conscript was a member of the Militia and during

which he could be recalled to the Regular Army if necessary. It appears that the initial conscripts and volunteers for the NVA did far in excess of their two years, since a 'state of emergency' existed and there was a reluctance to diminish the strength of the army until South Vietnam had been conquered.

The NVA eventually reached a strength of 480,000 men, and was organized into 14 divisions, each of about 12,000 men and supported by the usual artillery and tanks. There were, in addition, 10 independent artillery regiments, two independent armored regiments, and 20 independent infantry regiments, all of which were available as a reserve force to back up the divisions as and when required.

The distribution of this force is not entirely clear, due to the secrecy with which the NVA concealed their efforts during the war. The major portion, probably as many as 200,000, eventually formed the armed force in South Vietnam; but in addition there was a large component, estimated at about 75,000, in Laos and operating the Ho Chi Minh Trail supply route which kept the force in South Vietnam fed with munitions, and there was another force, estimated at 35,000 in Cambodia maintaining the sanctuary areas into which the armies in South Vietnam could fall back when threatened by US advances.

As the NVA increased in size and

progressed in skill, so it required more weapons; and as it came up against the American-supplied ARVN and later the US Army it suddenly realized that most of its weapons were now second-class. And when the US Air Force began bombing Hanoi and industrial targets in North Vietnam there was a sudden realization that the NVA was seriously deficient in modern antiaircraft defense. By 1964, according to conservative estimates from various sources, Soviet and Chinese aid to North Vietnam had reached about $800 million, most of which had been military equipment and the majority of that Soviet. With such an investment at stake, and with the prob-

ability of adding another pawn to the Communist chess-board, the Soviets responded to Giap's appeals and stepped up their provision of weapons. Until the Sino-Soviet split in 1960 shipments had come directly from Russia by rail, across China, but thereafter shipment was by sea to Haiphong, and Soviet freighters now began bringing in munitions in massive quantities.

The field armies benefitted first; out went the old M1944 carbines and the Simonov rifles, and the Kalashnikov AK47 became the universal infantry weapon. Sufficient were received for them to be shipped clandestinely to South Vietnam and used to arm most of

the guerrilla bands. The AK47 is considered by experts to be the most successful assault rifle ever made, and though no firm figures are avilable, it has been estimated that upwards of 20 million of them have been made and distributed throughout the world since its first appearance in 1951. Above all else, though, the AK47 has become the archetypical symbol of Communism; it is the standard arm of all the Warsaw Pact armies and it appears wherever Communist-backed 'nationalist' or 'revolutionary' groups flourish.

The old Degtyarev machine gun, which dated from 1926, used a rimmed 7.62mm cartridge which dated from the 1890s. The Simonov carbine and AK47 rifles, on the other hand, were chambered for a rimless 7.62mm cartridge with a thinner and shorter case which was developed at the end of World War II. The NVA had put up with the logistic problem of having to carry two kinds of ammunition for the basic infantry squad for long enough, and they now asked for, and received, a machine gun which fired

Left: A North Vietnamese supply column passes across a pontoon bridge in 1959. In spite of its primitive logistics set-up, North Vietnam kept the VC supplied throughout the Southeast Asia conflict.

Below left: A US airman is led into captivity in this staged propaganda photo.

Below: Vietnamese peasants assist in camouflaging a barbed-wire entanglement.

the same cartridge as the rifles. This was the 'RPD' ('Ruchnoi Pulyemet Degtyarova' = flexible machine gun designed by Degtyarev), a modern and efficient machine gun fed from a 50-round belt which was usually carried in a drum beneath the weapon. Weighing only 16lbs and with a rate of fire of 700 rounds a minute, it was far better than any comparable weapon the ARVN or US Army could produce and it became a highly-valued ambush weapon.

The increasing use of air support, and particularly of helicopters led to a considerable increase in the number of heavy machine guns deployed by the NVA and VC. These were two Soviet models, the 12.7mm DShK (Degtyarova Shpagina Krupnokalibernyi = heavy-caliber, designed by Degtyarev and Shpagin) and the 14.5mm KPV (Krupnokalbernyi Pulyemet Vladimirova). The former is roughly equivalent to the American 0.50 Browning heavy machine gun and was extensively used, mounted on a stand, for air defense, at which it soon gained a formidable reputation. The KPV was even heavier, having been

designed after World War II to take advantage of a particularly powerful 14.5mm (0.57 inch) cartridge originally developed for use in an anti-tank rifle. A heavy weapon – the gun alone weighs 108lbs – it was mounted on a wheeled trailer and used as a positional air defense gun; it was also mounted in twin and quadruple form, but these were usually to be found in North Vietnam guarding airstrips, bridges and similar vital spots.

The last problem facing the NVA was the American use of armor. Their anti-tank rifles, of Soviet origin, had been fine weapons in their day, but their day was long gone and although they could penetrate a modern APC they did little or no damage and they were useless against American tanks. The Soviets provided their RPG-2 rocket launcher as a replacement, and this had far more damaging effect against any sort of armor. Like many Soviet weapons it was an improved version of a captured German device, the famous 'Panzerfaust'. It consisted of a lightweight tube which had a pistol grip and trigger and a simple

sight. Into the front of the tube went a rocket-propelled grenade with a shaped charge warhead which was of 82mm diameter, much larger than the launch tube. When the trigger was pressed the rocket ignited and flew from the muzzle, a set of fins springing out to stabilize its flight. It had a range of about 150 yards, and could penetrate up to seven inches of armor plate.

The RPG-2 was followed in the late 1960s by the RPG-7, a much more formidable weapon. It resembled the RPG-2 in general form but used a somewhat different principle. The launcher tube carried a small cartridge which, when fired, kicked the rocket out of the tube and also released a short back-blast which balanced the recoil so that the firer's aim was not disturbed. After a second or two of flight a powerful rocket motor ignited and accelerated the rocket to its target. This method of launch was developed because a powerful rocket ignited in the launcher would have been burning as it left and would have injured the man holding the tube. Kicking the rocket out with a recoilless charge made

life safer for the firer and permitted the maximum rocket power to be incorporated. The RPG-7 had a maximum range of 500 yards and the much-improved shaped charge warhead could penetrate 12 inches of armor.

The NVA were familiar enough with the principles of recoilless weapons. The Chinese had given them a number of 57mm and 75mm recoilless rifles, some of US origin and some copied from the US design by the Chinese. These fired shaped-charge shells against armor and they were also useful as company support weapons because they were provided with high explosive shells and also white phosphorus smoke shells, though these latter were in short supply. The 57mm was out-dated by the early 1960s, since it no longer had any effect against modern armored vehicles, and it was dropped from use and replaced by a Soviet recoilless weapon, the B-10 82mm gun. This was a very light equipment, easily carried by two men or dragged on a light two-wheeled carriage, and it fired a fin-stabilized shaped-charge bomb from its smooth-bored barrel. As

an anti-tank weapon it was quite effective, with an engagement range of 500 yards or so and capable of penetrating nine inches of armor. With a high explosive/fragmentation bomb it became a good company support weapon, with a range of about 4000 yards.

The next requirement was mortars, since these are ideal jungle and guerilla weapons. They are light and portable, they have a high rate of fire, their high trajectory is ideal for dropping bombs behind protective cover and through tree-tops, and the sharp angle of arrival of the bomb guarantees a widespread distribution of blast and fragments. The two models adopted by the NVA were the 82mm M37 and the 120mm M43, both of Soviet design. The 82mm was a conventional 'Stokes' type of mortar, a smoothbored tube supported on a bipod with its base resting on a circular steel plate. It fired a seven pound bomb to a range of 3000 meters and a well-trained five-man crew could get 25 rounds a minute out of it.

The 120mm M43 was a powerful weapon which was virtually light artil-

lery. It can be moved easily by its own two-wheeled transporter, or it can be split into loads and mule- or man-packed. Unusually for a mortar it has a form of recoil buffer connecting the barrel to the bipod, so that the shock of firing is somewhat lessened and does not affect the sights. Firing a 34lb bomb to 6200 yards, it had a rate of fire of up to 15 rounds a minute.

Good as these mortars were, they were not always the best weapon for guerillas, since they had to be laboriously carried into position, together with their ammunition, fired, and laboriously taken away again, often under conditions of hot pursuit by US or ARVN troops. The Soviets had supplied a number of multiple rocket launchers for artillery use; these were of 107mm caliber and fired a spin-stabilized rocket to a range of about 5000 yards. It was realised that instead of using the truck-mounted multiple launcher tubes, it was

Below: A North Vietnamese Army truck convoy typical of those that passed along the Ho Chi Minh Trail to the South.

Above and below: Infantry of the North Vietnamese Army in action.

possible simply to lay the rocket on the ground, point it in the required direction, and ignite it by a battery and a short length of wire. If one wished to be more technical, it was possible to build a launching ramp from timber, sufficient to give the rocket its desired azimuth and elevation to hit a selected target with some degree of accuracy. The idea was rapidly taken up and put to use by guerillas, who could carry a 45lb rocket quite easily, build a simple ramp, fire the rocket at a US fire base, a large target hard to miss, and then decamp into the woods carrying nothing.

Artillery was an area in which the NVA definitely got the worst of it once the Americans arrived. The American

weapons were better, had longer range, and had a far more sophisticated and effective fire control system than anything the NVA could produce. Again, the answer lay in more modern weapons, discarding the old 76mm guns of wartime vintage and adopting the latest Soviet 130mm M-46, a surprisingly accurate weapon which fired a 73lb shell to a range of almost 30,000 yards. This was a formidable performance, but it had to be paid for in the weight and bulk of the gun, which at 19,000lbs was considerably heavier than the American 155mm howitzer.

The terrain conditions of Vietnam made towed artillery something of a burden; as we have seen, American towed

Above: North Vietnamese AA gunners man their 37mm cannon in 1965.

artillery was almost always lifted by helicopter unless there were good roads in the area it intended to emplace, and there was no time wasted in attempting to tow through jungle or across rough country. For that the Americans used self-propelled artillery, moving on tracks and capable of crossing virtually any terrain. Since the NVA had no hope of ever acquiring sufficient helicopters, or pilots, to lift their artillery they had to rely upon truck towing or man-handling when the going got too rough for the trucks. But they were helped out by Soviet-supplied self-propelled guns.

The Soviet approach to self-propelled artillery is (or was at that time – it may be changing in the 1980s) vastly different to that of Western nations. To the American or British artilleryman, self-propelled artillery means conventional indirect-fire artillery which just happens to be mounted on tracks for convenience in cross-country work and to allow it to maneuver with the armored formations it usually supports. It operates in exactly the same manner as towed artillery, occupies the same sort of positions, fires the same sort of missions.

The Soviets, on the other hand, were strongly influenced by German techniques in World War II and they adopted the German thinking of the time. This saw the self-propelled gun as a cheap substitute for a tank; for a tank chassis of given size, you could fit a turret with a gun of a certain caliber and the whole thing cost X marks. If you took the same chassis, abandoned the turret, built up the sides, and put in a gun of twice the caliber, you got two such 'assault guns' for the same price. This accompanied the assaulting infantry, firing as it went and acting in direct support to blast out any machine gun post, pillbox or other obstacle which threatened the infantrymen. This appealed to the Soviet tactical concepts, which always envisaged direct assaults with overwhelming numbers of men and guns, and they adopted the same system and have stuck to it ever since. As a result, the self-propelled guns which the NVA received were 'assault guns' in the Soviet/German sense rather than self-propelled field artillery in the Western sense. Instead of sitting behind the lines and using indirect fire to command a large area, they

accompanied the infantry and moved with them, in the front line, to take on direct-fire targets at point-blank range. Most Americans who saw them – and there were not that many – considered them as tanks and dealt with them accordingly; they had a low survival rate in the field.

The smaller model given to the NVA was the SU-76, a design dating from 1942. It was based on the chassis of the long-obsolete Soviet T70 light tank, stretched and widened, with the rear section built up into an armored box which carried a 76mm divisional field gun. It fired a 14lb shell to a range of 12,000 yards and could move at about 28mph on good roads. but its armor was less than one inch thick and its chances of survival in modern warfare rather slender. It appears to have been seen but rarely in Vietnam.

The larger model was the ISU-122, a more formidable equipment built from the chassis of the 'Josef Stalin 2' heavy tank and mounting a 122mm gun. The

fighting compartment was at the front of the vehicle, the engine and transmission at the rear, so as to require the minimum alteration from the tank layout. The gun fired a 55lb shell to a maximum range of 14,600 yards, though in practice this range was never utilized. The armor was of 110mm thickness at the front and 90mm on the hull sides, much thicker than the SU-76 and comparable with contemporary battle tanks, making the ISU-122 a formidable assault weapon. It was not very nimble, having a top speed of just over 20mph, but this was ample for its role of accompanying infantry in the attack. It was this model which was most often seen in Vietnam.

The T34 tank which the Soviets had originally supplied to the NVA were, by

Below: Women of North Vietnam's People's Militia return to work after a US air attack in November 1965.

Bottom: A wheel-mounted 75mm recoilless rifle captured from the Viet Cong is examined by US Marines.

Above: US Marines examine makeshift Viet Cong anti-aircraft guns captured during a sweep south of the Demilitarized zone.

the early 1960s, long in the tooth; they were probably the oldest tanks still in military service anywhere in the world. The Soviets had designed the T34 in 1939; had the 1940 Russo-Finnish War lasted another week, the T34 would have had its baptism of fire there, but in the event it had to wait for the German attack of 1941 to show what it could do. It proved to be the best all-round tank of the war, with a potent 76mm gun, wide tracks which gave it excellent cross-country performance in snow and mud, good armor and a reliable air-cooled engine. The fact that it was still in use in 1960 is testimony to its advanced design when it was introduced. But by 1960 it was no longer a match for American M48s and M60s, and the gun no longer had the performance to cope with such targets. The NVA had some T34/85 models, which were the same tank with an 85mm gun; this had a somewhat better anti-armor performance, but it was still the same obsolete tank and it was hampered by poor sights and fire control equipment.

To remedy this, the Soviets supplied the NVA with about 100 T54 and T55 tanks. The T54 was a lineal descendant of the T34, improved by the adoption of such ideas as torsion bar suspension, a transversely-mounted engine, better ballistic shaping of the hull (to deflect shot away from the tank) and a better-shaped turret, low and rounded. The result was a better protected, low-silhouette tank, though it weighed more than the T34 and was somewhat slower. Its gun was a 100mm rifled weapon of high velocity, firing a 35lb shot which could pierce six inches of armor at 1000 yards range. The T55 was an improved T54, as might be imagined, with a more powerful engine and modified transmission.

By Soviet (and Vietnamese) standards these were advanced tanks; by Western standards, less so. While their exterior shape was excellent, their mechanical reliability good, and their agility likewise good, from the offensive point of view they left a lot to be desired. The 100mm gun was a good basic design, and the turret now had electro-hydraulic power rotation instead of the hand rotation of the T34. But the optical sight was still poor, and there was no form of modern

fire control equipment. The turret revolved above the hull, but there was no 'basket' beneath the turret to hold the crew and rotate them at the same time; consequently they were required to shuffle around the tank floor as the turret moved, to avoid being hit by the gun breech and keep their action positions for loading and firing the gun. The T55 improved on this in a most unusual and unnecessarily complicated manner; a circular section of the tank floor, immediately below the turret, was connected to the turret rotation mechanism so that the floor revolved in sympathy with the turret, carrying the crew round. In later models of the T54 and all models of the T55 the gun was stabilized in the vertical and horizontal planes; this meant that once the gunner had laid his sight on a target, gyroscopic controls kept the gun pointed at the target irrespective of what movements the hull of the tank made. In theory this means that the gunner can engage targets while his tank is driving across country, but in fact this demands a very high degree of training and was rarely, if ever, seen employed by Vietnamese tanks. Normally they moved into position, stopped, took aim and fired; stabilization is theoretically a very good thing, but in practise it means nothing if the sights are not first-class and backed up by a modern computing fire control system with a laser rangefinder, and the NVA tanks had none of that.

The other Soviet tank supplied to the NVA in some numbers was the PT76 light amphibious tank. This was a more modern design, having first appeared in Soviet service in 1952. It is still in widespread use in Communist armies and is a somewhat angular tank mounting a modern 76mm gun in its turret. Lightly armored – a maximum thickness of 14mm – it is highly maneuverable and has the great advantage of being able to swim in any depth of water, being propelled by two water-jet units at the rear end. It can swim at about six mph, and the only preparation required is to erect the 'trim vane' at the front (which prevents water being swept over the hull) and switch on two electric bilge pumps to clear away the inevitable small leakage. The PT76 appears to have been more popular with the NVA – certainly

more of these were seen by US troops than were T54/55s – but they were very vulnerable to gunfire from US tanks.

Once the field armies were equipped, the next priority was to protect Hanoi and the other vulnerable areas of North Vietnam from American air attacks, and for this the Soviets shipped in massive amounts of air defense equipment. The first shipments were of anti-aircraft guns, fire control equipment and radar. For field forces and for the defense of airstrips and less important targets, the twin 37mm M1939 gun was provided. This is a thinly-disguised copy of the famous Bofors 40mm gun designed in Sweden in 1929 and subsequently used all over the world. The twin gun unit is mounted on a light four-wheeled trailer mount, and the guns are fed by clips of five rounds. Firing at a rate of 80 rounds per gun per minute, the M1939 has an effective ceiling of about 2000 feet and is purely an 'eye-shooting' weapon, using a simple correcting sight which compensated for the target's direction and speed to point the gun at the spot where shells and airplane ought to meet.

The next gun was the 57mm S-60, a design based on a German experimental weapon of World War II and one of the best light anti-aircraft guns of the postwar period. It was on the usual sort of four-wheeled mount, fired at 70 rounds per minute from four-round clips, and had an effective ceiling of about 12,000 feet. An optical sight was fitted, as was a telescope sight for firing at ground targets, but the 57mm was normally deployed as a battery and connected to a fire control computer and a 'Fire Can' tactical radar. The radar detected targets and fed their course and speed to the computer which then calculated the 'future position', ie where the airplane would be by the time the shell got up to its height. This was transmitted electri-

Top left: Viet Minh troops stage a triumphal entry into Haiphong – North Vietnam's chief port – after the defeat of the French Army at Dien Bien Phu in 1954.

Above left: An artillery unit of the North Vietnamese Army pictured in action.

Left: North Vietnamese anti-aircraft gunners man their 12.7mm heavy machine gun and keep watch for enemy aircraft.

cally to the guns and displayed on dials; the gunners matched pointers on the dials to set their guns in sympathy with the transmitted information and then opened fire.

The 37mm and 57mm guns were designed to deal with low-flying attacks; for high flyers it was necessary to use more powerful weapons, and these were the 85mm and 100mm guns. The 85mm M1944 was, in fact, the same gun as that used on the T34/85 tank, but on the usual sort of four-wheeled anti-aircraft mount. It fired a 21lb shell at a rate of about 15 rounds a minute to an effective

approaching the end of its service and about to be replaced by something better. The American army was never slow in bringing in a new piece of equipment to Vietnam in order to try it out in combat, taking precautions that it should not be exposed to the danger of capture, but certainly extracting as much useful information from it as possible before returning it to the USA for further development. The Soviets, on the other hand, always distrustful of their allies, were reluctant to allow their hands on anything really modern, even though the Vietnam war would have made a good

about 50 yards apart and connected to a fire control center. Two radars controlled the site; one was the 'Spoon Rest' surveillance radar which scanned the surrounding air space and gave early warning of the approach of targets; it had a range of about 170 miles. The second radar was the 'Fan Song' tactical radar which incorporated equipment to pick up and track the target when alerted by 'Spoon Rest', track the missile after its launch, and transmit correction commands to the missile.

The SA-2 missile used a solid-fuel booster to accelerate the rocket on

ceiling of about 30,000 feet. Like the 57mm it was provided with optical sights but rarely used them, being connected to a 'Fire Can' radar and a PUAZO-6/12 fire control computer. A fuze-setting machine on the gun mount was used to cut time fuzes to the length transmitted from the computer so as to burst the shells at the forecast point in the sky.

The 100mm gun KS-19 was a postwar Soviet design and an extremely powerful gun. It fired a 35lb shell at a rate of about 15 rounds a minute to a height of 45,000 feet. There is a powered fuze setter and a power rammer to assist in loading, and no optical sights are fitted, the gun being controlled entirely by a PUAZO-7 computer and 'Whiff' fire control radar. 85mm and 100mm guns were disposed around Hanoi and other important targets in considerable numbers.

It will have been noticed that in this listing of Soviet weapons transferred to the North Vietnamese, everything has been of a pattern either discarded by the Soviets or, if in service with them,

proving ground for all sorts of weapons. The reason for this is partly their inate distrust, and partly that such weapons as tanks and artillery were all based on well-known principles and, provided they tested out satisfactorily at proving grounds, their combat application could be fairly accurately gaged. But there was one class of weapon to which this did not apply; anti-aircraft guided missiles had never been used in combat by the Soviets, and they knew absolutely nothing of their actual performance in service conditions. When the gun defenses of Hanoi proved ineffective in halting American raids, the Soviets decided that here was an opportunity not to be missed; they would provide missiles and 'advisers' to the North Vietnamese defenses, and thereby learn a great deal about modern air defense techniques.

In June 1965 the first shipments of SA-2 missiles arrived and were set up around Hanoi; they were followed by more until by 1972 some 300 missile sites were in use. The missiles were deployed in batteries of six launchers, spread out

Top left: An unexploded American bomb provides instruction for young North Vietnamese volunteers in February 1970.

Above: A unit of the People's Liberation Army in Laos parades for a roll call in the summer of 1972.

launch, and a liquid-fuelled sustainer rocket which kept up its speed during flight. Once launched it had to be collected by the radar tracker during the first few seconds of flight. The radar then constantly monitored the missile's position and sent this information to a fire control computer. This was being fed with the position of the target, and it compared the two and decided upon the necessary flight correction for the missile to steer it to the target. This correction was then sent back to the radar and transmitted to the missile, where the guidance system moved the tail fin control surfaces accordingly. This constant check and correction was continued until the missile hit the target. The 285lb explosive warhead had multiple fuzing which permitted either impact detona-

Above : Soldiers of the Communist Pathet Lao man a Soviet-supplied 57mm anti-aircraft gun in Laos.

Above: North Vietnamese AA gunners train their twin 37mm gun. This weapon has a rate of fire of 180 rounds per minute.

tion, controlled firing by signal from the radar, or automatic detonation when the missile passed within lethal distance of the target. The missile had a range of about 35 miles and a ceiling of about 60,000 feet.

On paper the SA-2 should have been all-conquering, and certainly the first few weeks of its employment saw a number of hits on American B-52 bombers. But American electronic counter-measures equipment was rapidly brought into use, which effectively blinded the radars and confused the control system, causing the missiles to wander off course and out of control. Then the US began using radiation-seeking missiles which would lock on to the radar beam emitted by the fire control equipment, fly down it and destroy the radar. Between these two, and with intensive precision bombing of the missile sites, the SA-2 rapidly lost its edge.

Armies are made up of men and equipment. Both can be of varying quality, but whilst good soldiers can often work miracles with second-rate equipment, the finest equipment in the world is wasted if the soldiers are incapable of using it. The North Vietnamese soldier was efficient so long as he was operating simple equipment, but his record with more sophisticated weapons is a poor one. There was scarcely any confrontation of US armor by NVA armor, and on the rare occasions that this did happen, the NVA armor invariably came off worst; in plain terms, the NVA soldier was incapable of obtaining the maximum efficiency from what was, to him, a sophisticated weapon system. On the other hand, when it was simply a matter of rifle and machine gun fire, ambushes, forced marches and hand-to-hand combat, the North Vietnamese soldier was working well within his capabilities and

proved to be resourceful and dangerous. The fact remains, however, that the victory of North Vietnam over South Vietnam was political, not military, and assessments of the capabilities of the NVA should take this fact into consideration.

The Vietnam People's Army Air Force (VPAAF) was never a very large air arm, but it nevertheless performed creditably against the more numerous and better equipped United States air forces. Formed in May 1955 after the French withdrawal, North Vietnam's air arm was slow to develop. It was not until February 1964 that the first fighter regiment was formed and this unit first saw action in the spring of 1965. Organization was along Soviet lines, with inter-

Below: According to North Vietnamese propaganda, this AA unit had shot down 162 US aircraft by the end of 1969.

ceptor units formed into regiments and operating under the close supervision of ground controllers. Pilot training took place in the Soviet Union and units were then formed in China, where they carried out combat training before flying to their operational bases in North Vietnam. The greater number of fighter aircraft flown by the VPAAF were MiG-17s and MiG-21s manufactured in the Soviet Union. However, from 1968 onwards these were supplemented by Shenyang F-6s, pirated versions of the Soviet MiG-19 built in China.

As the war in Southeast Asia progressed, there was a steady build-up of North Vietnamese fighter units. In mid-1966 there were 65 aircraft in service, comprising a single squadron of Mach 2 MiG-21s and some 50 older, subsonic MiG-17s. A year later the VPAAF had 100 fighters, nearly half of them MiG-21s. When the United States launched its Linebacker I campaign against the North in May 1972, the opposing fighter force then numbered some 200 aircraft, 93 of them MiG-21s, 33 Shenyang F-6s and the remainder MiG-17s and MiG-15 advanced trainers. The VPAAF's fighters flew from nine airfields (later increased to 13), many of them grouped around the Hanoi-Haiphong region. The most important of these were Phuc Yen, Kep, Gia Lam, Cat Bi and Kien An. During the 1968 bombing halt, airfields in the south of the country were improved to permit jet operations and in the final offensive against the South in 1975 airfields at Khe Sanh and Dong Ha south of the former demilitarized zone were available to the VPAAF. In the event the North Vietnamese 'fighter force played little part in the 1972 or 1975 offensives. The small bombing unit, equipped with only five or six elderly Ilyushin Il-28s, was equally inactive and there is no record of it operating against the South. North Vietnamese airfields were off limits to United States bombers until 1967 and airfields in China were used by the VPAAF with impunity throughout the conflict.

The North Vietnamese fighter pilots were often highly-skilled and a number of them performed outstandingly well. Captain Nguyen Van Bay was the VPAAF's first ace and he scored at least seven kills. Colonel Tomb was another

successful North Vietnamese fighter pilot with over a dozen victories to his credit when he died in combat with the US Navy's ace Randy Cunningham in 1972. Twenty-two North Vietnamese pilots received the award of Hero of the Vietnam People's Army and by the end of the conflict the VPAAF had engaged in over 400 air combats and claimed 320 American aircraft destroyed. According to US sources only 92 American aircraft were lost in air combat over North Vietnam and the North Vietnamese lost 193 aircraft.

The oldest and in some ways the least effective fighter operated by the North Vietnamese was the MiG-17. This was a development of the MiG-15 of Korean War vintage with a thinner and more sharply swept wing and an elongated fuselage. These modifications together with the introduction of an afterburning engine (the 7500lb thrust Klimov VK-1F) resulted in a faster aircraft than MiG-15. Nevertheless the MiG-17 was unable to reach Mach 1 in level flight.

Wing span was 31ft 7in, length 36ft 4in and maximum take-off weight 14,750lb. Maximum speed at 10,000ft was just over 700mph, rate of climb was 12,800ft per minute and service ceiling was 55,000ft. Armament consisted of three nose-mounted NR-23 23mm cannon. The fighter's shortcomings in comparison with the American Mach 2, missile-armed F-4 Phantom necessitated special tactics. The MiG-17s flew at low altitude, defending North Vietnamese airfields or covering likely approach and withdrawal routes used by US strike fighters, and they usually operated in pairs. They sought to lure their opponents into turning fights in which they could quickly gain an advantage over the F-4 and the far less maneuverable F-105. However, unless heavily laden with ordnance, both US fighters could outrun the MiG-17.

Below: North Vietnamese infantrymen aim the highly-effective RPG-7 rocket launcher, with its armor-piercing warhead.

Above: A North Vietnamese Army T-54 tank crashes through the gates of the Presidential Palace in Saigon, signalling the fall of South Vietnam in April 1975.

The Shenyang F-6 did not reach North Vietnam until after the 1968 bombing halt and so did not see as much action against US strike aircraft as the MiG-17 or MiG-21. Only eight fighters of this type were claimed as victims by US fighter pilots, in contrast to more than sixty claims each for MiG-17s and MiG-21s destroyed. In performance it fell mid-way between the latter two fighters. A twin-engined aircraft powered by RD-9 turbojets producing 7,150lb of thrust with afterburning, the F-6 reaches a maximum speed of Mach 1.4 and has a maximum rate of climb at sea level of 22,600ft per minute. Service ceiling is 57,000ft. The F-6's swept wing spans 29ft 6in, length is 41ft 4in and maximum take-off weight is 19,600lb. A heavy gun armament of three NR-30 30mm cannon is carried, two of these weapons being mounted in the wing roots and the third in the starboard lower fuselage. Although an elderly design by the late 1960s, the F-6 was a very agile fighter by virtue of its low wing

loading and its highly-effective gun armament could be supplemented with two Atoll infra-red guided missiles.

The principal opponent of the US air forces for most of the conflict was the MiG-21. Several versions of this small and agile delta-wing fighter served with the VPAAF, including the MiG-21F clear-weather interceptor armed with a single 37mm cannon and two Atoll AAMs, and the later MiG-21PFMA with all-weather capability and an armament of twin-barrel 23mm cannon and four Atolls. Maximum speed of the MiG-21 was Mach 2, with an initial rate of climb of 36,000ft per minute and service ceiling of 59,000ft. Power for the later versions operational in Vietnam was provided by a Tumansky R-11 producing 13,700lb thrust with afterburning. Dimensions included a wing span of 23ft 6in and length of 48ft, with a maximum weight of 21,600lb.

When the MiG-21s first appeared over North Vietnam in 1965 they carried only cannon armament and so they sought to engage their opponents in dogfights so that they could bring these weapons to bear. However, despite some success against flak-damaged aircraft straggling behind the fighter escort, these tactics

were not fully effective and the VPAAF was losing four MiGs for every US aircraft shot down. With the introduction of missile armament and improvements in North Vietnamese ground control, more effective high-speed, hit-and-run tactics were developed.

Ground controllers would direct pairs of MiG-21s into a position behind the American strike force from where they began a high speed attack run, launching their Atoll missiles and then, having reached a speed of more than Mach 1.4, they zoomed above and away from the US formation. In comparison with the US F-4 Phantom, the MiG-21 was more maneuverable and could accelerate more quickly at subsonic speeds at any height. It had the same advantages at supersonic speeds above 25,000ft. Conversely the F-4 was faster and more maneuverable at supersonic speeds below 25,000ft. Finally the F-4 was nearly twice the size of the MiG-21 and its engines produced a distinctive smoke trail of black exhaust making it far easier to see. However, in the contest for air superiority the VPAAF were the losers, as for every American aircraft that they brought down two to four of their own fighters were destroyed.

AIR
SUPPORT &
INTERDICTION

At the peak of the American involvement in the war in Southeast Asia a daily average of 800 sorties was flown by fighter-bomber aircraft operating in support of ground forces. Three out of every four sorties launched from airfields in South Vietnam were of direct assistance to the troops in the field – the great majority of the missions being for close air support (CAS) and tactical airlift. About half of the CAS sorties were flown by the United States Air Force, with one-third of the effort coming from aircraft of the US Marine Corps and the remainder from the Vietnamese Air Force. Additional close air support was available from the attack aircraft of the US Sixth Fleet, operating from their carriers in the Gulf of Tonkin, although they chiefly flew against targets in North Vietnam or the Ho Chin Minh Trail. During such emergencies as the Tet Offensive and the siege of the Khe Sanh in 1968 the close air support effort was greatly expanded.

Over half of the close air support sorties flown in a day were pre-planned, so that the pilots could be briefed in advance and the aircraft armed with ordnance suitable for their target. For example, 500lb or 750lb bombs were most effective against troops sheltering in fortified bunkers or beneath a dense canopy of jungle, whereas cluster bombs or napalm were better suited to troops in the open. However, not all demands for close air support could be anticipated and for this reason a number of fighter-bombers were held on ground alert. They were armed with a variety of ordnance, so that any target could be dealt with. Once a request for air support was received, an alert flight of two or four aircraft was scrambled and arrived over its target within forty minutes. If the need for aerial fire power was so urgent that a quicker reacton time was needed, then aircraft already in the air could be diverted from their original targets. On the rare occasions when ground forces were so vulnerable that their requests for close air support had to be met immediately, then an airborne alert was flown over their area. However, as this expedient was wasteful of fuel and resources, it was only sparingly used.

Close air support sorties were very precisely controlled, at any rate in theory. A single Tactical Air Control Center co-ordinated all combat aircraft throughout South Vietnam. It monitored each mission and could divert any airborne sortie onto a new enemy contact or scramble aircraft on ground alert. The actual direction of CAS missions was delegated to Direct Air Support Centers, which were attached to each army corps. The US Marine Corps had their own control organization. Once the tactical fighters reached their target area, they came under the direction of a forward air controller (FAC). The FAC would brief the fighter pilots on the tactical situation and mark the target with smoke rockets for the fighters' attack.

The workhorse of the close air support effort in Vietnam was the North American F-100 Super Sabre. This tactical fighter-bomber entered USAF service in 1956 and first went into action over South Vietnam in 1965. (An earlier F-100 detachment to Thailand had seen combat over Laos in 1962). By 1967 the F-100 – usually known as the Hun – was the most important CAS aircraft in the theater of war and the planned reequipment of Air National Guard units in the United States with this fighter was delayed to keep the combat squadrons up to strength. The F-100D version, which with its two-seat F-100F derivative was the subtype of the Hun most widely used in South Vietnam, was a Mach 1.3 fighter with a range of 1500 miles. Armament comprised four 20mm M39 cannon (reduced to two on the F-100F) with 200 rounds per gun and bomb load was up to 7500lb. This load could be made up of a wide variety of weapons, including free-fall and retarded bombs, cluster bombs, napalm tanks and unguided air-to-ground rockets.

Apart from daylight CAS missions, the Huns flew similar sorties by night, using the light of flares to pick out target. This was a primitive method of target acquisition, which made great demands on the skill and stamina of the pilots involved and it was said that any pilot carrying out one of these hazardous 'Night Owl' missions could be sure of receiving a Distinguished Flying Cross in reward. Other roles found for the F-100 included leading formations of bombers on Combat Skyspot raids over North Vietnam, using special ground-directed radar bombing equipment to signal the release of ordnance in bad weather when the target was obscured or at night. High speed forward air control over North Vietnam where the slower FAC types used in the South would be very vulnerable, was another task undertaken by the Hun. The two-seat F-100F also pioneered the 'Wild Weasel' missions against North Vietnamese SAMs.

Overleaf: A USAF B-57 bomber departs on a night interdiction mission.

Below: The most effective tactical reconnaissance aircraft of the Vietnam War was the RF-4C Phantom.

Above: The B-57 Canberra bomber served throughout the Vietnam War; an EB-57E electronic warfare aircraft is pictured.

Right: A-7D Corsair II attack aircraft began operations with the 354th TFW at Korat in Thailand late in 1972.

The multi-role McDonnell Douglas F-4 Phantom was also used for close air support in South Vietnam, although its primary importance was as an escort fighter and fighter-bomber operating against targts in the North. The F-4 could lift a bombload of 9000lb and could carry a rapid-fire 20mm cannon mounted on the fuselage centerline or an underwing stores station. The USAF's F-4E model of the Phantom, introduced into combat early in 1969, had a built-in 20mm Vulcan multi-barrel cannon. Impressive though this armament was, the Mach 2 Phantom was really too fast and unmaneuverable aircraft for striking at the fleeting targets presented by the Vietcong or North Vietnamese Army units operating in South Vietnam.

A jet aircraft better suited to such con-ditions was the Vought A-7D, which reached Southeast Asia in October 1972. A subsonic, single-seat aircraft, the A-7D was equipped with a highly-accurate, computerized bombing and navigation system, which gave the aircraft a true all-weather capability independent of direction by ground radar units. Armament comprised a single 20mm M61 Vulcan cannon with 1000 rounds of ammunition and bomb load was up to 20,000lb (although 15,000lb was more usual). The A-7D represented the best available compromise between the fast jet CAS aircraft such as the F-100 and F-4 and the slow, piston-engined attack aircraft which had operated so effectively against the guerrillas in South Vietnam. Although the A-7D came late into the Southeast Asia conflict, it did carry out CAS sorties in Laos and was used over North Vietnam during the Linebacker II air strikes in 1972. The last bombing strike of the Southeast Asia conflict was flown by an A-7D over Cambodia on 15 August 1973.

The dependence of the USAF on fighter bombers for close air support and air strikes against the North highlighted the virtual disappearance of the light bomber from the air force inventory in the 1960s. Aircraft of this class had been particularly successful as interdiction aircraft in World War II and in the Korean War, but in Vietnam only the remaining 1950s vintage Martin B-57s served in the light bombing role. The B-57 was the USAF's version of the British Canberra and curiously enough the British version too saw service in Viet-

Left: An F-100 pulls away from its target after dropping napalm. The Super Sabre was the first jet fighter to reach Vietnam.

nam when the Royal Australian Air Force despatched its No 2 Squadron flying English Electric Canberra B Mk 20s to Phan Rang in April 1967. Between that date and the Australians' withdrawal in May 1971, the Squadron flew nearly 12,000 bombing sorties, many of them being precision daylight bombing attacks over the South. In USAF service the 8th and 13th Tactical Bombing Squadrons were the main operators of the B-57 in Southeast Asia, flying daylight bombing missions over South Vietnam and night interdiction and strike missions over the Ho Chi Minh Trail and North Vietnam. The B-57 carried a crew of two and its performance included a cruising speed of 420 knots (or Mach 0.74) and a combat radius of 824 nautical miles. Its built-in armament was four 20mm M39 canon, each with 200 rounds of ammunition, and bomb load options included four 750lb bombs in the internal bomb bay, with a further four on wing pylons. Flare pods could be carried on the wing stations for night missions, as could 2.75in or 5in rocket pods.

As the American policy of 'Vietnamization' gained ground towards the end of the 1960s, such close air support aircraft as the piston-engined A-1 Skyraider and the light jet Cessna A-37 Dragonfly assumed greater importance, as it was these machines which the South Vietnamese air force could most easily be trained to maintain and to fly. It was also considered that such aircraft were better suited to carry out counter-insurgency operations than were the more sophisticated jet fighter-bombers. However, it is interesting to note that whereas A-1s and A-37s flew 2055 and 8305 combat sorties inside South Vietnam in 1969, figures for the F-100 and F-4 were 52,699 and 19,185 sorties.

Below: This bomb-laden A-37B Dragonfly served with the 14th Special Operations Wing at Bien Hoa air base, South Vietnam.

The Cessna A-37 Dragonfly was a relatively straightforward conversion of the USAF's T-37 standard basic jet trainer to the light attack mission. As the A-37 retained the trainer's side-by-side seating arrangement for the two crew members, it was ideal for converting the relatively inexperienced South Vietnamese pilots from piston to jet engined combat flying. By the spring of 1969 three South Vietnamese fighter squadrons were flying the A-37 and at peak strength after the American withdrawal nine VNAF squadrons were equipped with more than 200 Dragonflies. Max-

imum speed of the A-37B was just over 500mph and its range with a maximum weapons load of 4700lb was 4600 miles. A GAU-2B 7.62mm minigun was installed in the nose and there were eight underwing weapons hardpoints.

The other jet aircraft type operated by the VNAF was the Northrop F-5 single seat fighter. The initial production version, the F-5A Freedom Fighter, was powered by two General Electric J85-GE-13 turbojets, each rated at 4080lb thrust with afterburning, giving a maximum speed of Mach 1.4 at 36,000ft. Armament included two AIM-9 Side-

winder air-to-air missiles mounted on wing-tip launch rails and two M39 20mm cannon with 280 rounds of ammunition per gun mounted in the nose. However, it was primarily as a ground attack aircraft rather than an air superiority fighter that the F-5 was to be used in Southeast Asia. Its small (4000lb) warload was a distinct limitation in this role, but this disadvantage was offset by the fighter's excellent handling and performance characteristics and its ease of maintenance. A USAF evaluation unit, the 4503rd Tactical Fighter Wing, flew 12 F-5As in combat over South Vietnam and Laos between October 1965 and March 1966 in order to assess the type's suitability for full-scale deployment to Southeast Asia. As a result of the findings of this deployment, code-named Skoshi Tiger, the F-5A was supplied in quantity to the VNAF. Eventually eight South Vietnamese squadrons operated F-5s and these included a number of the more powerful F-5E Tiger II with a 7,000lb warload.

The early close air support operations of the VNAF were flown exclusively by piston-engined attack aircraft, which often carried a USAF instructor pilot as well as the Vietnamese crew. One of the aircraft types supplied to the South Vietnamese in early 1962 was the North American T-28D. Together with combat instructors of the USAF's air commando training squadron codenamed 'Jungle Jim', the T-28s formed the basis of the VNAF's 2nd Fighter Squadron. Originally a piston-engined basic training aircraft for the USAF and US Navy, the T-28D counter-insurgency aircraft was modified to carry an armament of two 0.50 caliber machine guns, plus 1800lb of rockets, bombs or napalm. Powered by a single 1,425hp Wright R-1820-56 radial engine, the T-28D had a maximum speed of 360mph and a normal take-off weight of 15,600lb. The T-28 operated both by day and on night armed reconnaissance missions over South Vietnam. It also equipped the air forces of Laos, Cambodia and Thailand.

An altogether more powerful piston-engined attack aircraft was the Douglas A-1 Skyraider, which operated not only with the VNAF but also with attack squadrons of the US Navy and the

night attack missions against truck convoys in Laos until finally withdrawn from operations in 1969.

At the other end of the scale from the attack sorties flown by venerable piston-engined warplanes were the Arc Light operations mounted against targets in South Vietnam by Strategic Air Command's eight-engined B-52 strategic bombers. The first of these missions was flown from Guam in June 1965 and two years later a second force of B-52s began

Left: A string of 750lb bombs dropped from a B-52 during an Arc Light sortie explode on suspected VC positions.

Below: Helicopter gunships were able to provide fire support much closer to friendly forces than could the jet fighter bombers.

USAF's Special Operations Squadrons (formerly Air Commando Squadrons). Nicknamed the Spad (partly as a pun on the US Navy's AD designation for the aircraft and because to jet-age aircrew it seemed as venerable as the World War I Spad biplane fighters), the A-1 first saw action from US Navy carriers during the Korean War. The aircraft was perfectly adapted to conditions in Southeast Asia, carrying a warload of up to 8000lb plus four 20mm cannon in the wing. Its massive 2700hp R-3350 radial engine gave the A-1 a maximum speed of 318mph and a range of some 3000 miles with external tanks. An assortment of bombs, rockets, napalm or auxiliary fuel tanks could be carried on no less than fourteen underwing hardpoints, with a further stores pylon on the fuselage centerline. It is hardly surprising that the rugged and robust Skyraider was in great demand from the air forces engaged over Southeast Asia. A large number of surplus US Navy Skyraiders were passed to the USAF and VNAF and apart from CAS missions, they flew escort to the combat rescue helicopters. Two especially noteworthy feats of arms are associated with the Skyraider. Major Bernard Fisher of the 1st Air Commando Squadron landed on a forward airstrip as it was being overrun by the enemy to pick up a fellow pilot who had just force-landed there. This gallant rescue under fire was recognized by the award of the Medal of Honor. The second incident involved four US Navy

A-1s of VA-25 operating from USS *Midway*. On 20 June 1965 the Skyraiders were intercepted by a North Vietnamese MiG-17, which they succeeded in out-maneuvering and shooting down.

It was not however the A-1 Skyraider which was the oldest combat aircraft to see service in Southeast Asia. This honor belongs to the World War II vintage Douglas A-26 Invader, which saw early service in Vietnam with the air commando's 'Farm Gate' deployment in 1962. In 1964 these machines were grounded due to metal fatigue in the wing structure, but a refurbished Invader, the B-26K later redesignated A-26A, reentered service in 1966, assigned to the 609th Special Operations Squadron at Nakhon Phanom in Thailand. These aircraft flew

operating from U Tapao in Thailand, from where they could reach their targets in South Vietnam without needing to refuel in flight. The B-52D was specially-modified for these operations, enabling it to lift a massive conventional bomb load of 108 500lb or 750lb bombs. The main objectives of the Arc Light sorties were North Vietnamese Army/ Viet Cong troop concentrations and supply dumps. Whenever possible the B-52s' bomb runs were directed by Combat Skyspot ground-based radars, which were able to achieve a greater degree of accuracy than the aircraft's own bombing radar. The effects of a formation attack by B-52s was quite literally devastating. It was claimed by General William Westmoreland, the commander of the US Military Assistance Command Vietnam that B-52 strikes were the decisive factor at the siege of Khe Sanh, as they prevented the North Vietnamese from concentrating their troops for a large-scale assault on the base. The accuracy of the large bombers' delivery was such that they were bombing within 300 yards of friendly troops. However, such an extravagant application of military fire power inevitably attracted critics who claimed that there was little evidence that the B-52s were doing more than spectacularly cratering the Vietnamese countryside.

Both the US Navy and the US Marine Corps operated inside South Vietnam, the latter being responsible for the air support of Marine ground units. The US Navy regarded air operations over South Vietnam as a warming-up period for newly-arrived aircrew. An aircraft carrier beginning a deployment to the Gulf of Tonkin would begin its combat cruise on Dixie Station, before moving North to Yankee Station and operations over North Vietnam. The Marines flew from airfields ashore, the first of which was established at Chu Lai, fifty miles south of Da Nang, in 1965. The Douglas A-4E Skyhawks which the Marines flew from this base used jet-assisted take-off techniques and wire-arrested landings to enable a fully-laden aircraft to operate from a 3600ft runway. Such operations from what the Marines termed a SATS (Short Airfield for Tactical Support) enabled an air base to be constructed and operational within a month of starting work on it.

The Marines made extensive use of the A-4 Skyhawk for close air support missions and the all-weather A-6 Intruder and F-4 Phantom fighter-bomber were also flown in support of ground forces. In fact the Marine Corps' F-4 saw no air-to-air combat throughout the conflict, although Marine pilots on exchange postings to US Navy squadrons engaged North Vietnamese fighters from time to time and scored a number of kills. A notable contribution from the Marine air units was the Intruders' operations in support of the Khe Sanh defenders when bad weather had grounded most other aircraft.

An important complement to the air support operations in South Vietnam was the forward air control system.

Above: Infantrymen crouch behind cover as the air strike that they have requested goes in. The aircraft is an F-4 Phantom.

Flying a relatively slow observation aircraft – initially the Korean War vintage Cessna 0-1 Bird Dog, later more-powerful, twin-engined Cessna 0-2s or North American Rockwell OV-10 Broncos – the forward air controller or FAC was the link between the often high and fast flying attack aircraft and friendly forces on the ground. The FAC sought out targets which a fast jet would have never seen and then marked them for attack, firing smoke rockets. In contrast to World War II and Korea, when forward air control was only necessary for close air support sorties in the vicinity of friendly troops, the Vietnam War required FACs to carry out visual reconnaissance over South Vietnam to detect traces of an elusive enemy. Consequently there evolved two types of FAC operation. One was in support of friendly troop movements and so FACs were assigned to all major ground combat units. The other was concerned with daily reconnaissance over a single Vietnamese province, so that an experienced FAC familiar with his territory could immediately spot any unusual ground activity which might betray the presence of an enemy unit. He could then call in a ground patrol to investigate.

The elderly Cessna 0-1 Bird Dog carried the burden of FAC duties for much of the war. A two-seat, high wing observation aircraft, it had first entered service with the US Army in 1950. The Bird Dog was powered by a single 213hp Continental 0-470-11 air cooled engine,

which gave it a maximum speed of 115mph and a range of 530 miles. The aircraft was unarmed apart from its marker rockets and the crew's sidearms. Its most serious faults were its lack of endurance and reserves of power, plus the total absence of protection for the crew and fuel tanks.

The Bird Dog's successor, the Cessna 0-2, was a conversion of the civil Skymaster. Its performance was a considerable improvement over the 0-1, as its twin 210hp Continental I0-360-C piston engines (mounted in an unusual arrangement, with one as a tractor and the other a pusher) provided considerably more power. Maximum speed was nearly 200mph and range was increased to 1080 miles. Furthermore the underwing marker rockets could be supplemented by a 7.62mm minigun pod, giving the FAC a chance to fight back against groundfire. Yet with all these positive virtues, the 0-2 still lacked armor protection for the crew and the aircraft's vital systems.

The most effective FAC aircraft in Southeast Asia proved to be the OV-10A Bronco – perhaps not surprisingly, as it had been designed specifically for this task in the light of early experience in Vietnam. Powered by two 715shp T76-G-10 turboprops, the Bronco had a maximum speed at sea level of 280mph and a maximum range of 1140 miles. The

Above: A formation of UC-123s spray defoliant. The aim of Project Ranch Hand was to deny the VC jungle cover.

Left: A formation of South Vietnamese Air Force A-1E Skyraiders fly over the Mekong River during a close air support sortie.

Inset far left: The Cessna O-2 forward air control aircraft offered many improvements over the earlier O-1.

Inset left: This O-1 served with the South Vietnamese Air Force's 23rd Tactical Wing, based at Bien Hoa near Saigon.

pilot's and his observer's view from the cockpit was outstandingly good and both crew members had armored protection. In addition the OV-10 had a built-in gun armament of four 0.30 caliber machine guns and its 3600lb weapons load could include offensive ordnance as well as marker rockets. The first USAF Broncos reached Vietnam during 1968 and in addition to serving with air force FAC units, the type equipped US Marine Corps observation squadrons and a special US Navy squadron – VAL-4, the Black Ponies – which protected convoys on the Mekong River as well as seeking out enemy forces in the region.

One of the most controversial opera- tions of the Vietnam War was Project Ranch Hand – the spraying of defoliants over jungle areas to deny the Vietcong both the forest covering which they re- lied on for concealment and the crops of rice and manioc planted by them to eke out the meager rations reaching them from North Vietnam. The spraying air- craft were modified Fairchild C-123 Pro- vider tactical transports, designated UC- 123Bs, the first six of which deployed from Clark Air Base in the Philippines to South Vietnam in November 1961.

Another unusual air force commit- ment was the psychological warfare role. This involved dropping leaflets and safe- conduct passes over Vietcong-held areas urging the guerrillas to surrender to Government forces. An alternative ploy was to broadcast taped messages from loudspeaker-equipped aircraft. Two air- craft types were modified for this role with the air commando squadrons: the Helio U-10 Courier, a single-engined, high-wing monoplane with good short take-off and landing characteristics, and the venerable Douglas C-47, the most widely used transport aircraft of World War II which has seen service in virtual- ly every postwar conflict.

Modified C-47s were also widely used for reconnaissance duties over South Vietnam. The EC-47 variants were equipped for electronic reconnaissance, monitoring the wavebands for enemy radio transmissions which would betray the positions of Viet Cong camps. Camera-equipped RC-47s also served in South Vietnam. Reconnaissance over the defended airspace of North Vietnam was carried out by RF-101 Voodoos and RF-4C Phantoms. The less demanding reconnaissance missions fell to older types, such as the RB-26 version of the Invader (deployed to Vietnam in the ear- ly 1960s), and the RB-57, which pioneered the use of infra-red photogra- phy in the combat theater. A highly-unusual approach to the problems of locating an elusive guerrilla enemy re- sulted in the Lockheed YO-3 Q-Star, which was evaluated in South Vietnam in 1970. The aircraft was basically a two-seat glider, modified by fitting a 100hp Continental 0-200-A engine (later re- placed by a 185hp Wankel rotary). The engine was muffled so that the Q-Star could operate at altitudes down to 100ft at night without alerting the enemy. Its principal reconnaissance equipment was an infra-red sensor.

Night air operations were of consider-

able importance during the Southeast Asia conflict and nowhere were they more vital than over the Ho Chi Minh Trail. This network of jungle tracks led from North Vietnam through southern Laos and thence into South Vietnam. It was along this route that the greater part of the supplies and reinforcements needed by the North Vietnamese Army and Viet Cong units fighting in the South had to pass. Consequently it became the prime target for USAF interdiction operations. In many ways this was an unsatisfactory state of affairs, not least because the Ho Chi Minh Trail offered few of the tempting bottleneck targets such as bridges and railroad marshalling yards which figured so prominently in the target planning of World War II and Korea War interdiction campaigns. Because, with the exception of the passes from North Vietnam into Laos, there were no obvious choke points, the USAF's interdiction sorties had to be directed at the vehicles moving along the Trail.

In theory at least, there was an alternative interdiction strategy to picking-off truck convoys, which could be easily dispersed to avoid offering a single vulnerable target to air attack. This was to strike at the North Vietnamese supply lines much nearer to their sources. Little in the way of arms and munitions was produced in North Vietnam. The war supplies needed for the guerrilla war in the South were imported from Communist allies, either by sea to the port of Haiphong, and various other North Vietnamese harbors, or by rail from the People's Republic of China. If these supply routes could be blocked, then the North Vietnamese war effort would be appreciably weakened. However, political restrictions ruled out attacks that could provoke the Chinese into entering the war and for similar reasons the sea mining of North Vietnam's harbors was ruled out until the very end of the conflict. There remained the North Vietnamese rail and road systems, which were in fact attacked to good effect. Yet because of the various bombing halts and other restrictions placed on the USAF's target planning, a consistent and continuous interdiction campaign against the North's transportation systems and logistics centers proved to be

Top: A C-130E air drops supplies. Up to 16 one ton palletized loads could be released from the Hercules in one mission.
Above: ARVN troops board a C-130 Hercules; the transport's standard troop load was 92, but on operations this could be exceeded.
Left: The most warlike role undertaken by the Hercules in Southeast Asia was that of gunship, an AC-130A being illustrated.

Overleaf: The C-5A Galaxy (left) and C-141A
Starlifter bore the brunt of stategic airlift in
the later years of the war.
Overleaf, inset top: The B-52D bomber was
modified to lift 108 750lb bombs.
Overleaf, inset bottom: C-7A Caribou
transports could carry 32 troops.
Above: An OV-1 Mohawk is armed with gun
and 2.75in rocket pods on underwing pylons.
Left: The C-123 Provider flew transport
missions and sprayed defoliants.
Below left: An Army Chinook is airlifted to
Vietnam aboard a C-124 Globemaster II.

impossible. Thus it was only by harras-
sing the truck convoys along the Ho Chi
Minh Trail that the USAF was able to
maintain a continuous pressure on the
Communist supply system.

Interdiction on the Ho Chi Minh Trail
almost inevitably involved night sorties,
as most truck movement took place in
darkness and vehicles on the move were
more easily detected than were well
camouflaged truck parks. Ninety per
cent of all trucks destroyed by American
airmen on the Trial were engaged in
darkness. Therefore the first problem of
the interdiction campaign was the location of targets. This problem was solved

on early operations by the interdiction aircraft themselves – typically B-57s operating in pairs. One aircraft would drop flares, while the other bomber prepared to attack. This procedure was quickly refined so that a flare-dropping transport aircraft – a Fairchild C-123 or Lockheed C-130 Hercules – accompanied the attack aircraft to illuminate their targets. The business of flare dropping was inevitably hit-or-miss, as all the night interdiction team could do was to select a likely segment of the Trail to illuminate and hope that their flares would catch trucks out in the open.

Following these early attacks on the North Vietnamese supply routes to the South, a variety of tactics was developed to improve the efficiency of interdiction sorties. One expedient was the training of South Vietnamese ground reconnaissance teams, which were flown by helicopter into the Laos/South Vietnam border areas with the objective of locating enemy truck parks and supply dumps, onto which they could then direct air strikes. B-52 strikes were directed against various parts of the Trail by day, as were missions by F-100 and F-105 fighter bombers. Control of the bomber strikes was by Combat Skyspot ground radar, while the fighter bombers were directed by FACs and by airborne command post C-47 and C-130 aircraft.

However, it was the refinement of night attack techniques which was to pay the greatest dividends over the Trail. One approach resulted in the deployment of the B-57G night intruder, which was fitted with a powerful attack radar, low-light TV and forward-looking infrared, all of which could detect targets under cover of darkness (and in the case of the infra-red sensor, even under camoufalge). Once detected the target could be marked by a laser designator for attack by laser-guided bombs. The bomb run could be entirely automatic, as a computer processed the data from all sensors and directed the pilot into his bombing run. The B-57G was thus a highly-efficient night interdiction bomber, which could operate independently by locating, marking and then attacking its own targets. However, such results were not achieved cheaply. The development costs of the system were high and only sufficient B-57G conversions were produced to equip a single squadron. Similarly, although laser-guided bombs were very accurate (it is claimed that 80 per cent of the bombs dropped by B-57Gs fell within 15ft of the aiming point), they were costly to use against the average interdiction target.

A far more cost-effective system for night interdiction proved to be the gunship. Gunships were converted transport aircraft equipped with a heavy side-firing armament of rapid-fire machine guns and cannon. The weapons are aimed by the pilot flying a carefully banked turn around his target, so that it remains the center of his cone of fire. The first gunships were modified Douglas C-47s, officially designated AC-47Ds and unofficially dubbed Puff the Magic

Below: An AC-119G gunship of the USAF's 71st Special Operations Squadron flies over the Mekong River in 1968.

Dragon, or Spooky after the aircraft's radio call-sign. The AC-47D's side-firing armament comprised three six-barrelled, rapid-fire 7.62mm miniguns, each capable of firing 3000 or 6000 round per minute according to the rate of fire selected. If all three were fired at once – rarely done in practice – the 18,000 rounds per minute rate of fire would quickly exhaust the 24,000 rounds of ammunition carried. Up to 45 flares could be carried for target illumination, these simply being tossed out of the open cargo hatch by a crew member.

Two other transport aircraft types were converted into gunships. The AC-119G was built as a replacement for the AC-47 and was armed with four minigun pods and with a computerized fire-control system. However, more special-ized gunships intended specifically for truck-hunting along the Ho Chi Minh Trail were the AC-119K and AC-130 variants of the Hercules. The AC-119K added two M61 Vulcan rapid-fire 20mm cannon to the machine gun armament of the G. It was also fitted with two 2850lb thrust GE J85 auxiliary turbojets in underwing pods. Target acquisition was assisted by infra-red, radar and low-light TV, plus image-intensifying night observation sights.

The AC-130s were even more exten-sively equiped. Early AC-130As carried

Right: A US Marine Corps A-4 Skyhawk makes a rocket assisted take-off from a Short Airfield for Tactical Support (SATS).

four 7.62mm miniguns and four 20mm Vulcan cannon, later changed to two miniguns, two Vulcans and two 40mm Bofors cannon. Yet the ultimate in gunship armament was only reached with the AC-130H, which carried a 105mm howitzer in place of one of the Bofors. A wide range of avionics was fitted to acquire targets for the AC-130's awesome battery of guns. These in-cluded a search radar with moving target indicator, infra-red, low-light TV, a searchlight and flare dispensers. Perhaps not surprisingly these gunships were considered to be the USAF's most successful truck killers.

A rather different approach to the problems of night interdiction in South-east Asia produced the Project Black Spot NC-123K conversions of the Pro-vider transport. Only two aircraft were modified, but both saw combat service over the Trail and inland waterways, operating out of South Vietnam and Thailand. Although the NC-123Ks car-ried much the same range of sensors as the gunships – forward-looking radar, FLIR, LLTV and laser designator/ rangefinder – their armament compris-ed cluster bomb units (CBUs) rather than guns. The CBUs were stored in the aircrafts' cargo holds and dispensed through chutes fitted to the rear cargo ramp. In spite of problems with the sen-

sors and with accurate weapons delivery, the two Black Spot aircraft accounted for the destruction of more than 400 trucks and 50 sampans.

Shore-based naval air units played an important part in the interdiction cam-paign, not only by guarding against arms and supplies being ferried into South Vietnam by sea, but also by operating over the Ho Chi Minh Trail. The Navy had its own gunship, the AP-2H version of the Neptune patrol bomber. This car-ried the usual range of sensors, including radar, FLIR, LLTV and night observa-tion scopes. Armament was a mixture of high explosive and incendiary bombs, 7.62mm minigun pods, all carried underwing, and twin 20mm cannon in the tail turret. Over 200 sorties were flown by the four aircraft assigned to VAH-21 which operated from the mas-sive base at Cam Ranh Bay.

Another version of the Neptune, de-signated OP-2E, operated with VO-67 from Nakhon Phanom in Thailand. Its role was to sow seismic and acoustic sen-sors along the various tracks of the Ho Chi Minh Trail. This activity, part of Project Igloo White, was intended to provide accurate targeting information for the interdiction aircraft. As well as the Navy aircraft, USAF Skyraiders, Sikorsky CH-3 helicopters and F-4D Phantoms were used to drop the sensors,

which if they were to be of any use had to be placed with extreme accuracy. Once the sensors began to pick up indications of enemy movement, they transmitted this data to an airborne relay station – often a high-flying Lockheed EC-121, although the Beech QU-22 pilotless drone version of the Bonanza lightplane was specially developed for this work. The data was then retransmitted to a ground control station, the Infiltration Surveillance Center, where it was collated with other intelligence sources and used for target planning.

The seaward flank of South Vietnam provided an alternative infiltration route to the Ho Chi Minh Trail and for this reason it was continually patrolled by Navy aircraft. Operation Market Time, as this activity was code named, was a tedious and often unrewarding activity, which could involve flights of up to 12 hours duration. The greater number of these patrols were flown by Lockheed P-2 Neptunes, later joined by the newer P-3 Orion. However, early coastal surveillance was carried out by the Martin P-5 Marlin flying boat, this being the last operational use of such craft by the US Navy.

If coastal patrols were almost invariably uneventful, the same was not always true of tactical air transport operations in South Vietnam. The aircraft types operated in this role included the veteran Douglas C-47, the first USAF transport aircraft to be deployed to South Vietnam, in November 1961. Their early missions included the resupply of US Army Special Forces detachments, which were scattered among remote outposts throughout the country. The VNAF also flew the C-47, but because of a shortage of trained Vietnamese pilots, 30 USAF pilots (the Dirty Thirty) were assigned to the two VNAF transport squadrons in 1962. Air transport within South Vietnam was especially valuable at a time when Viet Cong guerrillas frequently cut the main highways and ambushed military truck convoys. For cargoes too bulky for the C-47, the VNAF received a number of elderly C-119 transports.

One of the most widely-used tactical transports of the conflict was the Fairchild C-123 Provider, a twin-engined aircraft modified in the C-123K version with two 2850lb-thrust J85 auxiliary turbojets in underwing pods to improve take-off performance. The Provider was considered to be obsolescent by the end of the 1950s and was on the point of retirement from the regular USAF. However, the Vietnam conflict gave it a new lease of life, as the Provider's ability to operate from short and unsurfaced airstrips made it the ideal transport for supplying remote garrisons and Special Forces posts. Until the mid-1960s, when the C-130 Hercules began to operate within South Vietnam, the C-123 was the most important tactical transport of the war and it served throughout with both the USAF and the VNAF.

The larger and more capable Lockheed C-130 Hercules was powered by four 3750shp Allison T56 turboprops, giving it a payload of some 15 tons and a

Below: An A-26A Invader of the 609th Special Operations Squadron based at Nakon Phanom in Thailand.

Left: A napalm-armed F-5A pictured during the Skoshi Tiger evaluation in Vietnam.

Above: A French Beaver evacuates wounded.

range of well over 2000 miles. At the peak of USAF involvement in southeast Asia in 1968, 15 C-130 squadrons were supporting the war, either flying supplies into the combat theater or carrying out missions within South Vietnam.

Cargo and personnel transport represented the day-to-day work of the transport forces, this effort being coordinated by the Airlift Control Center at Tan Son Nhut airfield near Saigon. However, more active military airlift operations were mounted from time to time. For example in early 1967 during Operation Junction City C-130s participated in the only battalion-strength parachute assault of the conflict. Air resupply sorties to airstrips under enemy fire were far more frequent. In May 1968 Lt Col Joe M Jackson landed his C-123 on the airstrip of the Special Forces camp at Kham Duc after it had been overrun by enemy forces in order to evacuate a three man combat control team. He accomplished this rescue in the face of intense mortar and machine gun fire, earning the award of the Medal of Honor for his gallantry.

The siege of Khe Sanh by North Vietnamese forces during the first four months of 1968 provided the tactical airlift forces with one of their greatest challenges. The 6000 man Marine Corps garrison defending the outpost was totally dependant on air resupply of ammunition and food. For much of the siege, Communist shellfire denied the transports the use of Khe Sanh's runway so that supplies had to be air dropped and bad weather over the beleagured outpost often hampered air supply operations. Yet these difficulties were surmounted and between 21 January and 8 April USAF tactical airlift units delivered 12,400 tons of supplies to the garrison. The greater part of the airlift was

Above: F-100 Super Sabres bore the brunt of the USAF's massive close air support effort in South Vietnam.

Left: The F-105 Thunderchief primarily operated against North Vietnam, but it did fly some missions over the South.

provided by C-130s, which flew 90 per cent of the sorties.

In addition to the USAF and VNAF transport units operating in Vietnam, the US Army and US Marine Corps also flew a proportion of the transport sorties required to support their ground forces. The Marines standard transport aircraft was the KC-130F, a version of the Hercules which could operate both as a tactical transport and as an air refuelling tanker. The Army's standard transport was the de Haviland Canada C-7 Caribou, a twin-engined aircraft with a maximum payload of 8740lb, which was able to operate from short, unsurfaced airstrips close to the battle area. The US Army's intention was that the Caribou

would transport men and supplies to a forward airstrip as near to the battle area as possible. Thereafter helicopters would distribute their loads and passengers to the front-line combat units. However, this method of operation trespassed on the USAF's preserves, as that service and not the Army was responsible for the tactical airlift mission. Consequently, following a ruling by the Joint Chiefs of Staff, the army's six Caribou companies were transferred to the USAF, becoming squadrons of the 483rd Tactical Airlift Wing. Eventually a number of Caribou were passed on to the VNAF and a squadron of the Royal Australian Air Force also operated the type in Vietnam.

An account of air transport operations in Southeast Asia would be incomplete without mention of Air America, the CIA-funded airline which flew clandestine transport and supply missions in Laos and Cambodia. Typically such missions would involve food and arms shipments to Vang Pao's Meo tribesmen in Laos, with C-7 Caribous or C-123s flying the cargo into Vientiane. From there it was airlifted up-country in such elderly transports as C-47s or Curtiss C-46 Commandos. Air America also flew more modern STOL (short take-off and landing) transports, such as the Pilatus Porter, and various helicopters.

The American military involvement in Southeast Asia was supported by a massive strategic airlift effort, which in 1967 alone involved Military Airlift Command (MAC) transport aircraft flying 210,000,000 miles and carrying sufficient personnel to man 85 infantry divisions. In 1965 the mainstay of the command was the piston-engined C-124 Globemaster, which could lift a 50,000lb payload over a range of 4050 miles at a cruising speed of 230mph. In practice this meant that a C-124 operating from Travis Air Force Base in California to

Saigon would take nearly two weeks to complete the round trip.

The C-124 was by far the most numerous strategic transport in USAF service in 1965, equipping 21 squadrons. The rather more capable, turboprop-powered C-133 Cargomaster could achieve the same mission with a greater payload and making fewer stops en route. However, its cruising speed of some 310mph was inadequate and only three squadrons of MAC flew this aircraft. The remainder of the Command's squadrons flew the C-130 Hercules, or the C-135 Stratolifter, the military equivalent of the Boeing 707 airliner. Neither of these aircraft was entirely suited to the Southeast Asia airlift task,

Below: The dramatic effect of fire from an AC-119 gunship operating at night.

as the C-130 lacked range and speed, while the C-135 had a limited capacity.

The efforts of MAC's regular squadrons were supplemented by transport units of the Air Force Reserve and Air National Guard. Civil airline charter also contributed to the airlift effort. However, it was not until a new generation of turbofan powered strategic transports – the Lockheed C-141 Starlifter and the same company's C-5 Galaxy – entered service that the strategic airlift situation began to improve.

The C-141 Starlifter began to operate into South Vietnam in August 1965 and all 284 had been delivered to the USAF by the end of 1968. Powered by four 21,000lb thrust Pratt & Whitney TF33 turbofans, the Starlifter could carry 67,000lb of cargo over 4000 miles. The cargo hold could accommodate 154 pas-

sengers; or fitted as an aerial ambulance, 80 stretcher patients and 16 seated passengers. From 1965-72 the C-141 flew some 6000 casualty evacuation sorties.

In 1969 MAC began to operate the massive C-5A Galaxy and flights to Vietnam began in August 1971. Powered by four 41,000lb thrust TF39 turbofans, the Galaxy could lift a 164,000lb load over a distance of 3000 miles at a speed of 450 knots. Its 120ft long cargo compartment could accommodate 98 per cent of the Army's equipment items including tanks and self-propelled howitzers. Used as a troop transport, it could accommodate 270 men in the cargo hold, plus 75 on an upper deck. The C-5A was particularly active in ferrying supplies to South Vietnam in the time between the North Vietnamese invasion in March 1972 and the ceasefire of January 1973.

THE RIVER WAR

Overleaf: A river patrol boat of the US
Navy's River Patrol Force 116 moves at high
speed on the Saigon River in 1967.

The riverine warfare which was so characteristic of the fighting was merely an extension of a similar conflict which had gone on between the French and the Viet Minh from 1946 until the surrender of Dien Bien Phu eight years later. This was inevitable, for the rivers are the key to the country. Nearly 90 per cent of the usable communications are in the form of rivers or canals; during the monsoon the roads quickly become impassable, and in the dry season guerrilla activity against the road network proved easy.

The Mekong Delta is a flat, low-lying area covering nearly a third of the country which had become the Republic of South Vietnam in 1954, although clearly it had formed a much smaller part of Indo-China when it had been in French hands. Being covered by rice paddyfields and swamps, and intersected by numerous rivers and drainage canals it is in many areas almost impassable to vehicles of any sort. Progress on foot is difficult, too, and against a determined force of well-armed guerrillas an army

could take weeks to cover only a few miles. The annual rainfall in the Delta is 80 inches, and much of it falls in the summer.

The central part of South Vietnam, known from the French days as Piedmont or the foothills is drier and less intersected by watercourses, but further north the narrow coastal plain reverts to flat valleys, marshland and paddyfields. Here the rainfall is a mere 65 inches per year, falling mainly during the monsoon in September, October and November. In the monsoon season cross-country movements become even more difficult, and even flying becomes dangerous, with poor visibility added to all the other hazards.

To the French under Vice-Admiral Ortoli the problem was quite simple. Control of the coast gave freedom of access and prevented the enemy from using them freely, while control of the inland waterways gave access to the very heart of the country. In a remarkably short space of time the French Navy

assembled a force of ex-Japanese junks and river launches, supplemented by Landing Craft Assault (LCAs) and Landing Craft Vehicle and Personnel (LCVP) from the British base at Singapore. They were rearmed with whatever weapons came to hand, including tank turrets and light anti-aircraft guns such as 40mm Bofors and 20mm Oerlikons. The basic unit became the *Dinassault* or River Assault Division, and these units fought many bloody close-range battles.

The 1000 miles of coastline from the 17th Parallel to Cambodia were thus part of the deadly inheritance which passed to President Kennedy when he took office in 1961. Indeed, many of the techniques painfully learned by the French were quickly taken up and adapted by US forces. In fact after the French withdrawal in 1954 the South Vietnamese forces had taken over the craft belonging to the *Dinassault* groups, and these forces were steadily augmented under the original Kennedy-Johnson policy of large-scale aid without intervention.

Left: The US Navy's patrol air cushion vehicles could move at speed over water, swamp, or flat land at will.

Below: Viet Cong prisoners are led ashore from a US Navy patrol air cushion vehicle. These craft began operations in 1966.

Left: A 40mm Bofors gun at action stations aboard a French patrol craft during operations against the Viet Minh in 1953.

Below: A monitor boat from the US Navy's River Assault Flotilla One uses its flame-throwers against VC positions.

Above: The three man crew of a US Navy skimmer boat keep a sharp look out for signs of Viet Cong activity.

Below: A squad of US Marines is carried aboard a river patrol boat. More than 400 of these craft saw service in Vietnam.

When in April 1965 President Johnson agreed to send in the troops the way was clear to provide US naval forces as well. The biggest headache was the delta of the Mekong River and its neighbouring coastal waters, through which some 50,000 junks plied their trade. Some of these junks were inevitably smuggling weapons and supplies to the Viet Cong, but others were peaceful, and to sort one from the other was almost impossible.

To patrol the inland waters the US Navy set up Task Force 116, the River Patrol Force, under Captain Burton B Witham Jr and ultimately responsible to the Commander of US naval forces in South Vietnam. The code-name for the operation was Game Warden, and dur-

Below: Assault support patrol boats and armored troop carriers move against a VC position on the Cho Gao Canal, June 1969.

ing the next ten years this flotilla was to grow to some 750 vessels.

The US forces were supplied with about 425 River Patrol Boats (PBRs). They were built in three series, 8-ton fiberglass craft 31-32ft long and driven by waterjets. With a twin .50cal machine gun mount forward and a single .30 aft they were capable of quiet high-speed operation in less than three feet of water. The waterjets were driven by twin diesels, pumping water through an intake in the keel then discharging through nozzles in the stern.

The principal advantage of this mode of propulsion is that it does away with vulnerable propellers and rudders.

Despite the attention paid to the de-

sign of the PBRs they did not find favor with the experienced veterans of riverine warfare, who preferred the slower but heavily armored landing craft left behind by the French. These were mostly adapted Landing Craft, Mechanized (LCM) and Landing Craft, Vehicle and Personnel (LCVP), whose hulls had originally been built in the United States during World War II.

The principal requirement was to protect crewmen and gunners from small arms fire and fragments from grenades and mortar bombs. To supplement the old French craft a new series of 'river monitors' was created, starting with the conversion of 24 LCM(6) from 1964 onwards. Armament varied, but typically it included an 81mm mortar or a pair of M10-8 flamethrowers, a 40mm Bofors gun, a 20mm Oerlikon and two .50 machine guns. Twin diesels drove them at 8 knots, ample for the job they were to do. From this concept was developed a much more powerful monitor, armed with a 105mm howitzer, two 20mm guns, three .30inch machine guns and a pair of 40mm grenade-launchers. As before the propulsion was twin diesels. What made these monitors unusual was a specially developed form of armoring. To keep down weight and at the same time keep out fragments closely spaced bars were used, and they had the advantage of coolness as well. Like the 24 ex-LCMs, nearly all the 42 improved monitors were handed over to South Vietnam between 1965 and 1970 as part of a Vietnamization programme.

Mention should also be made of the River Patrol Craft (RPC), which in fact predated the PBRs. They had welded steel hulls drawing 3½ feet, and a typical armament was twin .50inch machine

Top left: A crewman of an armored troop carrier mans his M60 machine-gun during a river patrol operation.

Above left: Members of the Vietnamese Mobile Strike Force aboard their airboat on the Mekong River in April 1970.

Left: The skipper of a river patrol boat aims a flaming arrow at a bamboo hut, which conceals a Viet Cong bunker.

Right: US Marines are embarked aboard river patrol craft during a sweep of the Ca Mau area in April 1969.

guns in a revolving mount forward, a twin .30inch machine gun aft and a single .30 above the conning position. Out of the total of 34 built most were handed over to South Vietnamese control on completion but a few were retained by the US Navy and put into service as river minesweepers.

The peculiar requirements of river warfare spawned other special types. Command and Control Boats (CCB) were needed to provide command and communications facilities for commanders of the River Assault Flotillas. They too were converted from the ubiquitous LCM(6), like the Armored Troop Carriers (ATC). These were needed to transport troops, wheeled vehicles, field artillery and stores, and many were fitted with a light steel helicopter deck over the open well deck forward. This enabled them to be used for casualty evacuation (casevac), and others were fitted with additional fuel tanks to allow them to refuel other river craft. In all over 100 ATCs were built, most of them passing under Vietnamese control in 1969.

One of the more unusual craft was the 'Mini ATC', a high-speed craft intended to land special forces and swimmers on raiding missions. Unlike most of the other riverine craft they were intended to make high speed, 28 knots, and one of the 15 built was driven by gas turbines. The aluminum hull was protected by ceramic armor to save weight, and at top speed they drew only a foot of water. A maximum of 20 troops could be carried.

Left: Members of a Vietnamese Popular Civilian Force unit are carried aboard a river patrol boat on the Vinh Te Canal.

Above: US Navy instructors explain the workings of a 20mm cannon to a South Vietnamese sailor.

In such a fragmented war it is difficult to single out highlights, and the river war in Vietnam suffered from its lack of whatever dubious glamor was associated with other parts of the American and South Vietnamese military operations. This is not to say that the military authorities in Saigon underrated the importance of controling rivers, but inevitably the endless repetition of small firefights merged into the background of violence. River forces played a significant part in the Chieu Hoi (Open Arms) operations, when Government forces sought to win over defectors from the Viet Cong. Moving up the canals and rivers, their crews were able to broadcast messages and distribute leaflets, all part of the PsyOps campaign to win hearts and minds.

As the pacification program got under way, so did the military effort. River craft were used frequently to carry Popular Force units from place to place, giving them a degree of mobility that would otherwise have been impossible. These operations became more successful when in December 1965 the Game Warden patrols began and small squads of US Marines were seconded to local Popular Force companies. In the following January the Marines began their Combined Action Program (CAP), initially in the Phu Bai region but soon extended to cover Da Nang. The Game Warden personnel began to arrive in numbers in February, at roughly the

Below: A sailor of the South Vietnamese navy mans a 0.50 caliber heavy machine gun mounted atop an 81mm mortar.

same time as the US Navy's first Sea, Air, Land (SEAL) platoon. These SEAL platoons were specially trained in counter-insurgency techniques.

As always in Southeast Asia the terrain was as much of an enemy as any human agency. In May two hovercraft (air-cushion vehicles) were sent out, a pair of Bell SK-5s. It was hoped that these craft would be able to cross inundated paddyfields, to lend added flexibility to the river operations, and although there was no doubting their capabilities their upkeep proved a headache. Although highly effective the hovercraft needed too much maintenance to endear them to the hard-working crews of what were now called River Assault Groups (RAGs).

To give some idea of the intensity of operations, by the end of 1966 there were 40 Game Warden craft in the waterways of Rung Sat, and twice that number were patrolling the Delta of the Mekong River. The arrival of detachments of US Navy Helicopter Support Squadron One's UH-1 Iroquois helicopters (better known as the Huey) was making a great difference to the work of

the patrol boats. These detachments had the colourful nickname of 'Seawolves', and were divided into two unit fire teams.

Recognition of the importance of the river operations came in February 1967, when Game Warden was made a separate command under Commander, Naval Forces, Vietnam (COMNAVFORV).

At the end of that month a new Riverine Assault Force, Task Force 117 was formed. The primary objective of TF117 was to take the offensive in the Delta and the Rung Sat marshes.

A typical river operation used a Mobile Afloat Force (MAF), which occupied floating barracks and supply craft known as the Mobile River Base (MRB). This group of craft would be protected by Assault Support Patrol Boats (ASPBs) and monitors, while US Army or ARVN units and artillery ashore provided cover. The other job of the ASPBs was to prevent the withdrawal of any Viet Cong by water, while ground-attack aircraft and helicopters provided air cover. The Armored Troop Carriers (ATCs) would put the assault force ashore, while other units

might be lifted inland by helicopter to prevent escape overland, forming the Blocking Force. Throughout all this the ASPBs and monitors would be providing close-in fire support, and another group of ATCs, including a floating aid station provided a Ready Reaction Force. This sort of operation in battalion strength was capable of fighting over an area of up to 15 square miles for a period of four to six days; at the end of that period the troops would normally be evacuated by helicopters or boats.

The first SEAL teams were organized into Mobile Support Team Two (MST-2) with six specially converted LCM(6) medium landing craft. The engines were heavily muffled, with the exhaust outlet under water, and even the engine room was soundproofed. The silhouette was lowered by cutting down parts of the ramp and superstructure, and the electrical system power was boosted to handle the extra communications equipment. Armor plating was provided for the ramp, well deck, engine room and steering position, capable of stopping a .50 cal machine gun at 100 yards' range. The engine room and steering position were also protected by bar armor and trigger

plates to deflect bazooka rockets and similar projectiles.

Armament of these early 'Mike boats' varied, mainly because many of the weapons were carried by whatever detachment was embarked, but the permanent weapons included a 106mm recoilless rifle forward and an 81mm mortar in the well deck. The second LCM was given a 7.62mm Minigun, a great advantage when suppressing hostile fire.

The first two LCMs were designated Heavy SEAL Support Craft (HSSC). Next to be converted were four 36ft LCPL Mk 4s. Although less elaborate than the LCM conversions they were treated in similar fashion, silencing of engines and protection against grenades and small arms fire. As before, weapons varied according to the mission, but a typical armament was two Miniguns, a 60mm mortar, two .50 cal machine guns, an M60 machine gun and a 40mm grenade launcher. Although more vulnerable than the HSSCs one of them returned to base with more than 200 hits. Only one of the 13 men aboard was unwounded and a 57-mm recoilless rifle shell had passed right through a fuel tank without exploding.

The personnel of MST-2 belonged to Boat Support Unit 1, from the Naval Amphibious Base at Coronado, California. Their tours of duty in Vietnam lasted 180 days, but as their highly specialized skills were in great demand they spent in all rather more time in Vietnam than many personnel on permanent duty.

In due course the first HSSC and MSSC craft were replaced by specially built craft. One of the LCMs sank while alongside a repair tender, and the other was found to be too worn out to be worth repairing, along with three of the ex-LCPLs. The fourth LCPL was about to be transferred to the South Vietnamese Navy in 1969 when she broke loose from her moorings and capsized. Primitive though these conversions were, they provided invaluable experience.

To enable the river forces to operate at maximum efficiency it was necessary to build them a proper base in the Mekong Delta. It was one of the unsung feats of the war, a two-year task for the US Navy's Seabees (Construction Battalions) and Army Engineers. To provide a large basin it was necessary to excavate riverside paddyfields, using hydraulic suction dredgers; sufficient mud was excavated to fill in a square mile of paddyfield. Nor was the operation unopposed and Viet Cong saboteurs succeeded in sinking one large dredger and two smaller ones before the large artificial island was completed.

Contemporary reports dwell on the physical exhaustion of working in the swamps and canals. The enervating heat and humidity recalled the operations around the Solomons in 1942-43, and it was necessary to pull out crewmen for a 'drying out' period after a while. Quite apart from the rigors of the climate there was the constant fear of an ambush.

The determination of President Nixon to end direct American involvement in the war meant an inevitable speeding up of the Vietnamization process, but there can be little doubt that the naval side was handled in such a way as to wipe out most of the gains of the previous four years. Hundreds of vessels were virtually dumped on the small South Viet-

Left: Riverine operations in Indo-China began with the French; these patrol craft of the French Navy were pictured in 1954.

Right: This US Army UH-1 Huey
operated from a small deck installed on
an armored troop carrier during 1967.

Right: This US Army UH-1 Huey
operated from a small deck installed on
an armored troop carrier during 1967.

Below right: The barracks ship USS
Benewah acted as a depot ship for armored
assault boats on the Mekong River.

namese Navy. The unfortunate Vietnamese had to cope with sophisticated
weapons and large-scale maintenance
and planning, almost overnight. It was
hardly a recipe for success.

Although belated attempts were made
to remedy the lack of training facilities
the South Vietnamese Navy was the least
likely of the three services to be able to
rise to the occasion. This implies no slur
on the South Vietnamese as people, but
experience in other countries shows that
naval training and an understanding of
the subtleties of combined operations
can only be inculcated over a long period
of time. Much more sophisticated navies
have had difficulty in assimilating these
doctrines, so it is hardly surprising that
there was an immediate falling off of
standards. Observers had already noted
that the structure of Vietnamese society
placed too much emphasis on family ties
and personal loyalty, at the expense of
professional skill and ability. All too frequently officers were promoted on
grounds of 'who they knew' rather than
'what they knew', and that combined
with a yawning gap between the compa-
ratively wealthy officer corps and the
peasant sailors, stifled what leadership
there was.

The Mobile Riverine Force was formally disbanded in August 1969 but in
its place was put a force manned by Vietnamese Marines aided by US Navy personnel. The value of the craft transferred
to the South Vietnamese was officially
put at $7.7 million, and the name Sea-
lords was chosen for the force, an
acronym for Southeast Asian Lake
Ocean River Delta Strategy.

There was plenty of work to do, for in
April 1970 the Saigon command launched a major offensive against Viet Cong
sanctuaries in neighbouring Cambodia.
The rivers were a vital supply-route
from Cambodia, and any incursion into
the country had to make full use of the
rivers. The Mekong itself flows from
Phnom Penh down through Vietnam,
and so a major effort was devoted to
keeping this route open. Even when in

May 1970 Cambodian forces failed to
open the Mekong River a large flotilla of
Vietnamese gunboats was sent upriver,
and this force succeeded in the task.
When the offensive subsequently failed
the river-route was equally important in
getting people out.

The withdrawal of American military
personnel in 1972 had its effect on the
river operations, although every effort
was made to provide continuing support. Little is know of the final struggle
but from what is known of the land

fighting it can be conjectured that the
South Vietnamese forces lost cohesion,
at first partially but later wholesale. After the fall of Saigon on 30th April, 1973
some of the fighting craft made their
escape but the majority fell into the vic-
tors' hands. The 1981-82 edition of
Jane's Fighting Ships contains a terse
note to the effect that many of these craft
may be non-operational for lack of
spares, but goes on to list no fewer than
563 ex-French and ex-American river
craft. They have no other memorial.

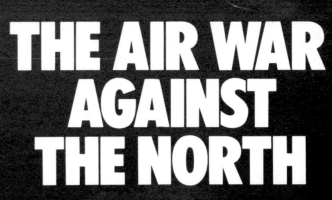

THE AIR WAR AGAINST THE NORTH

The United States' air war against North Vietnam began in August 1964 with retaliatory air strikes against torpedo boat bases. This response followed the Gulf of Tonkin Incident in which US Navy destroyers patroling in international waters were attacked by North Vietnamese PT boats. The attacks were launched by F-8 Crusaders, A-1 Skyraiders and A-4 Skyhawks operating from the carriers USS *Constellation* and USS *Ticonderoga*. Some 25 torpedo boats were claimed as destroyed or damaged, well over half the North Vietnamese fleet. Opposition was light as at this time the air defenses of North Vietnam consisted of little more than automatic weapons and small-caliber AA guns. However, the defenders did manage to bring down one A-4 Skyhawk, the pilot ejecting and being made prisoner of war. He was the first of some 600 airmen to fall into enemy hands, an indication of the improvements that were to be made to North Vietnam's air defenses and of the intensity with which the air war over the North was to be fought.

The air offensive against North Vietnam fell into two main campaigns, the series of Rolling Thunder air strikes be-

tween 1965 and 1968, which was followed by a bombing halt, and the Linebacker raids of 1972. Not only was the North immune from attack during the bombing halts, but numerous restrictions on targeting and engagement of enemy forces hampered the air offensive when it was in progress. For example, at one time in 1965 SA-2 missile sites and the airfields used by the MiG interceptors were off limits for attack, as were the areas around Hanoi and Haiphong. It is therefore hardly surprising that no dramatic results were produced by the air campaign with the exception of the final Linebacker II air strikes of December 1972 which brought a reluctant North Vietnam back to the negotiating table in Paris. The aims of the Rolling Thunder attacks were defined as the raising of South Vietnamese morale, punishing the Hanoi regime for its support of aggression in the South and reducing the flow of men and supplies entering the South. It was hoped that the air strikes would persuade the North Vietnamese to seek a negotiated settlement. However, President Johnson was determined that the air attacks would be limited in scope. Every major new target

had to be personally approved by him and he was anxious that neither China nor the Soviet Union should be drawn into the conflict. As a result the early attacks were largely limited to radar sites and bridges in the southern part of North Vietnam. It was not until mid-1965 that attacks on communications between Hanoi and the Chinese border were authorized.

The mainstay of the early bombing offensive against the North was the Republic F-105, officially named the Thunderchief but known in Southeast Asia as the Thud. The Thud was a large and heavy single-seat tactical fighter, which had been designed to carry out tactical nuclear strikes during a European War. Consequently it was fast at low altitude (maximum speed at sea level was Mach 1.25), and it could carry a heavy load of ordnance and range with maximum fuel was over 2000 miles. A maximum ordnance load of 16 750lb bombs could be lifted, but a more typical configuration was six 750lb bombs on the fuselage centerline, with 450 gallon auxiliary fuel tanks on the inner wing pylons and ECM jamming pods on the outboard stations. The Thud also car-

Overleaf: This US Navy F-4B Phantom is armed with two air-to-ground rocket pods underwing and a Sparrow air-to-air missile.

Left: A US Navy A-7A Corsair II pulls away from the target as its bombs straddle the Hai Duong highway bridge in 1967.

Below: A typical North Vietnamese SAM site, with SA-2 launchers ringing their radars, was photographed by a US Navy RA-5C.

Right: USS *Intrepid*'s catapult crew prepare an A-4F Skyhawk for launching during operations in the Gulf of Tonkin.

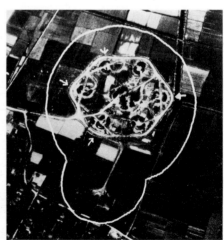

ried an internally mounted M61 Vulcan 20mm rapid-fire cannon with 1029 rounds of ammunition. This weapon could be used to good effect against enemy interceptors, no fewer than 22 MiG-17s falling victim to the F-105D's cannon. Another useful feature of the Thud was its two refuelling systems – a retractable probe and a boom receptacle – so that it could receive fuel from any tanker aircraft using either the US Navy's probe and drogue system or the USAF's boom and receptacle method.

Although Thuds carried out tactical air strikes over South Vietnam from time to time, the air war against the North was their true métier – so much so that the small mountain chain to the northwest of Hanoi, used by strike pilots to mask their approach to the North Vietnamese capital from enemy radars, has gone down in the history of the air war as 'Thud Ridge'. The F-105s were based in Thailand with the 355th Tactical Fighter Wing at Tahkli and the 388th TFW at Korat, operating over the southern panhandle of Laos and into the North. Thuds carried out more airstrikes into North Vietnam than any other USAF aircraft and consequently bore the brunt

of the losses. By the end of the 1960s enemy action and the normal wear and tear of accident and attrition led to the withdrawal of the F-105 from the air strike missions. So popular was this strike fighter with its pilots that at one time the reopening of the F-105 production line was considered in order to keep this doughty combat aircraft in service.

The F-105's successor in the strike fighter role was the F-4 Phantom, a multi-role fighter which had provided fighter cover for the Thuds from the earliest days of the conflict. Yet the F-105s disappearance from the strike squadrons did not mark the end of the Thud's fighting career, as it served on in the 'Wild Weasel' defense suppression role until the end of the Southeast Asia conflict and beyond. Yet if the F-105 was the preeminent strike fighter of the war, then the F-4 Phantom was without a doubt the leading MiG killer, assuming the mantle of the P-51 Mustang of World War II and the F-86 Sabre of Korea.

The McDonnell (later McDonnell Douglas) F-4 Phantom was originally designed as a two seat, twin engined carrier-based interceptor, with secondary attack capability, for the US Navy. The basic concept was so sound, that the F-4 was adopted by the USAF to meet its tactical fighter requirement of November 1961. This called for an aircraft capable of carrying out the close air support, interdiction and air superiority missions. The first production model of the Phantom for the USAF, the F-4C was very similar to the US Navy's F-4B, but was fitted with a boom receptacle for air-refuelling in place of the Navy's probe system.

The Phantom was powered by two General Electric J79 afterburning turbojets, each producing 17,000lb of thrust, giving the F-4 a maximum speed of over Mach 2 at altitude. Combat radius was around 400 nautical miles, ceiling was 55,000ft and maximum rate of climb at sea level 46,800 feet per minute. All of which added up to a useful performance for both air-to-air combat and ground attack missions. Armament comprised up to eight tons of munitions, which could include bombs, rockets, air-to-surface missiles and later in the war laser-guided or electro-optical 'smart' bombs. For air combat missions, the usual armament was four AIM-7 Sparrow medium range, semi-active radar homing missiles carried semi-recessed beneath the fuselage and four infra-red guided AIM-9 Sidewinder

Below: The US Navy's F-8 Crusader fighter was credited with the destruction of 19 North Vietnamese MiG fighters in combat.

Inset: A-7E attack aircraft are pictured on the flight deck of USS *Enterprise* at the time of the fall of Saigon in 1975.

short-range missiles carried on wing pylons.

The early models of the Phantom in USAF service, the F-4C and F-4D, had no built-in cannon armament, a serious shortcoming which was to hamper air combat operations over Sotheast Asia for much of the war. This was because a pod-mounted M61 Vulcan cannon had to be carried, ideally on the centerline station under the fuselage. However, as this position was usually needed for a 600 gallon auxiliary fuel tank, the gun pod was more often carried on a wing pylon. Any pylon mounting was unsatisfactory, because it lacked the rigidity of an internal gun mounting and therefore adversely affected the weapon's accuracy. Furthermore a pod-mounted system had only a limited ammunition capacity – some 1200 rounds in the SUU-16A pod

often carried by the Phantom – which was soon expended by the 6000 round per minute rate-of-fire of the M61 Vulcan cannon.

Other shortcomings in the F-4's design were revealed by early combat experience in Vietnam. The lack of a radar homing and warning system, which would alert the pilot to hostile enemy radars and warn him of impending attack by interceptors or surface-to-air missiles was one deficiency which called for urgent action. Another was the lack of electronic countermeasures capability, particularly against the guidance radar of the SA-2 Guideline surface-to-air missile. However, it was discovered that if a missile was spotted soon enough after its launch, a violently maneuvering F-4 could defeat its guidance system. The F-4D model Phantom, which had

Left: An A-7A Corsair II is positioned on an attack carrier's deck-edge lift. A-7s began to replace the A-4s from late 1967.
Below: An F-4J of Fighter Squadron 92 is about to engage USS *Constellation*'s arresting wire.

an improved bombing computer and a better gunsight, shared many of these problems. The need for multiple and triple ejection racks, which enabled one stores station to carry clusters of six or three bombs, was also an early problem.

Yet in spite of all these faults, the Phantom was basically a highly-effective combat aircraft, which was well liked by its crews. Many of the lessons of the Southeast Asia war were incorporated into the F-4E Phantom, which first flew in June 1967 and was deployed to Southeast Asia at the end of the following year, after a hurried flight test program because of the urgent need for the new fighter in the combat theater. Its important new features included a built-in cannon armament, with a 20mm M61 mounted in the nose. However, ammunition capacity suffered from this retrospective modification, as room could be found for only 640 rounds. Maneuverability was improved by fitting extendable slats to the wing leading edges. These were automatically deployed during high angle of attack maneuvers, providing the aircraft with 33 per cent more lift, thus greatly improving its turn radius and lessening the danger of the uncontrollable stall/spin. Although the pilots knew how to avoid this last danger, when flying heavily loaded fighters at low level in the heat of combat, it was easy to forget the warnings of training films and flying instructors and accidentally put the aircraft into a stall/spin from which there was little chance of recovery.

Six Phantom-equipped tactical fighter or reconnaissance wings served with the USAF in Southeast Asia. The 8th TFW, nicknamed the 'Wolfpack' and commanded in 1966-67 by that veteran fighter pilot Colonel Robin Olds, flew the F-4C and F-4D from Ubon Air Base in Thailand from December 1965 until the end of the conflict. The 12th TFW served in South Vietnam from November 1965 until November 1971, flying both the F-4C and F-4D. The 366th TFW, nicknamed the 'Gunfighters' initially served in South Vietnam with the F-4C, reequipping with F-4Es in 1969

and moving to Thailand in mid-1972. The 388th TFW at Korat in Thailand originally operated the F-105, but reequipped with F-4Es in 1969. Two tactical reconnaissance wings flew Phantoms, the 432nd TRW at Udorn Thailand operated a mixture of RF-4C reconnaissance aircraft and F-4D tactical fighters, whereas the 460th TFW operated RF-4Cs only and was based in South Vietnam from 1966 until 1971. During the Linebacker bombing offensive against North Vietnam in 1972 seven tactical fighter squadrons drawn from the United States based 31st TFW, 33rd TFW and 49th TFW were detached to Thailand for combat duty.

The Phantom accounted for the destruction of 107 enemy fighter aircraft during the Southeast Asia conflict, plus a further victory shared with an F-105. The F-4D was the highest-scoring subvariant with 44 kills, with the F-4C close behind with 42. During its much shorter combat career, the F-4E accounted for 21 enemy fighters, four of them MiG-19s and the remainder MiG-21s. Air-to-air missiles were responsible for most of the kills, 86 in all with the medium-range Sparrow scoring 50 of them. Gunfire claimed 15 victims and five opponents were simply maneuvered into the ground. Only three USAF aircrew scored the five or more victories which qualified them as 'aces' and significantly all three were F-4 crewmembers. The first USAF ace of the war was Captain Steve Ritchie, a pilot, while the other

two Captains Charles DeBellvue and Jeff Feinstein were backseat weapons system officers. They were all beaten to the honor of becoming the first American aces of the war by a US Navy Phantom crew, Lt Randy Cunningham and his backseater Lt (jg) Willie Driscoll.

The F-105s and F-4s had found it necessary to battle their way through the increasingly-effective North Vietnamese air defenses to reach their target. Not so the F-111 all-weather tactical fighter, which could use both low altitude and the cover of darkness to evade the defenses. The F-111 was produced in response to Secretary of Defense Robert S. McNamara's controversial TFX requirement for a multi-role fighter capable of meeting both USAF and US Navy requirements. There was nothing inherently implausible in this aim, as the distinguished combat career of the F-4 Phantom bears witness. Yet the F-111 proved to be totally unsuitable for carrier operations and did not go into US Navy service.

The USAF F-111A tactical fighter-bomber was a two-seat, twin-engined aircraft powered by two 20,00lb thrust Pratt & Whitney TF30 turbofans. Its maximum speed at altitude was Mach 2.2 and at low level it could reach Mach 1.2. Range carrying the maximum internal fuel load was 3300 nautical miles and up to 9000lbs of ordnance was carried on underwing racks. The F-111's variable-geometry wing gave it an excellent combination of both low and high speed

Right: A pilot's eye view as an A-6A takes on fuel from the buddy refuelling pack of a second Intruder.

handling characteristics and its advanced terrain following and attack radars used with an inertial navigation system made it possible to find and attack targets while flying at terrain-hugging height in darkness.

It was probably because of the many technologically advanced systems which the F-111 incorporated that controversy continued to follow this aircraft. Early in 1967 a small detachment of six F-111As was rushed to Southeast Asia to carry out a combat evaluation of the design. This early deployment of an untried warplane proved to be a mistake, as three of the F-111As taking part in this Combat Lancer deployment were lost in action. It was not until September 1972 that the aircraft was considered sufficiently combat-ready to be deployed to the Southeast Asia theater again. Then two squadrons of the US based 474th TFW were dispatched to Tahkli in Thailand for operations against North Vietnam and the Ho Chi Minh Trail. The concept of the F-111 was finally vindicated when these units mounted 20 air strikes over North Vietnam on 8 November 1972 in weather that had grounded the other aircraft of the strike force. More than 3000 mis-

sions were flown before the ceasefire of January 1973, for the loss of seven of the 52 aircraft deployed. Not only could the F-111s fly when other aircraft were grounded, but they could also do without the armada of support aircraft – fighter escorts, ECM escorts, defense suppression flights, tankers and airborne early warning aircraft – which had to accompany the F-105 and F-4 strike forces. Yet the F-111 was really ahead of its time and it was the aircraft of an earlier generation which bore the brunt of the bombing effort against the North.

It was not until the North Vietnamese spring invasion of the South in 1972 that the USAF's big stick – the B-52 bombing force – was wielded against the North. At this time there were a total of 138 B-52D and B-52G bombers deployed to the Pacific, 53 of them based at U-Tapao in Thailand and 85 at Andersen AFB on Guam. The eight-engined B-52 strategic bombers, with a range of 10,000 miles, a maximum speed of 660mph and a ceiling of 55,000ft, had a formidable conventional bomb load – up to 108 750lb bombs on the B-52Ds with the 'Big Belly' modification. Although operations against the North

represented only a small proportion (around six per cent) of the 126,663 B-52 combat sorties flown over Southeast Asia, the Linebacker II attacks against the heavily-defended Hanoi and Haiphong areas in December 1972 were undoubtedly the climax of the Stratofortress's war. In an eleven-day campaign more than 700 sorties were flown against rail yards, port facilities, headquarters and supply dumps. The defenders reacted fiercely, firing off virtually their entire stocks of SA-2 missiles and bringing down 15 B-52s for the loss of two MiG-21 interceptors which fell to the bombers' tail guns. However, by the end of the campaign on 29 December the North Vietnamese were ready to return to the negotiating table in Paris and the major objective of Linebacker II had thus been attained.

Among the highlights of the bombing campaign against the North was undoubtedly the battle of the bridges. Two of the key interdiction targets in North Vietnam were the Paul Doumer bridge

Below: The EF-10B Skynight (background) was used for electronic countermeasures, while the RF-8 flew photo reconnaissance.

Above: The first aces of the Vietnam war were US Navy pilot Lt Randy Cunningham and his backseater Lt (jg) Willie Driscoll.
Above right: The USAF's first ace in Vietnam was Captain Richard S. Ritchie, who flew F-4s from Udorn in Thailand.
Right: Col Robin Olds, a World War II ace, shot down four MiGs while commanding the USAF's 8th Tactical Fighter Wing.
Below: A MiG-17 in combat with US fighters.

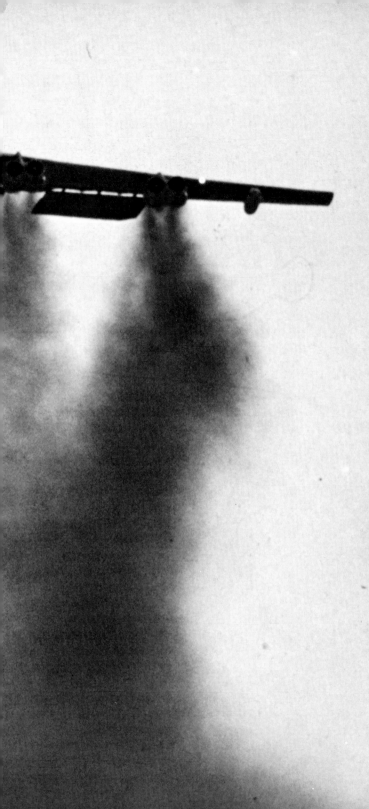

on the outskirts of Hanoi and the Thanh Hoa bridge further to the south. Yet the latter was a massive structure which proved able to withstand repeated assaults from conventionally-armed strike aircraft – and even a specially-devised 5000lb weapon which was dropped into the Song Ma River upstream of the bridge by a C-130 Hercules transport aircraft. The Doumer Bridge lay within the sanctuary area around Hanoi, in which bombing was forbidden until the summer of 1967, when the ruling was reversed. Accordingly a massive air-strike by three Thailand-based tactical fighter wings, the 8th TFW with F-4s and the F-105-equipped 355th and 388th TFWs, was mounted on 11 August. Running the gauntlet of intense fire from anti-aircraft guns and SAMS, the strike force streamed over the Bridge releasing their 3000lb bombs right onto the target dropping three spans into the Red River. By 3 October the Bridge had reopened to both road and rail traffic and so a second strike was mounted on 25 October, which again put it out of use until late November. Two final strikes in December were so successful that it was not until April that rail traffic resumed crossing the Red River. By this time President Johnson had imposed a bombing halt against targets north of the 20th Parallel effectively putting both bridges out of bounds again.

When bombing resumed in the spring of 1972 in retaliation for the North's invasion of South Vietnam, a new family of 'smart' munitions was available to the USAF for precision air attack. This included electro-optically guided bombs

Left: A USAF B-52 Stratofortress lifts off. B-52s operated from bases in Thailand and on Guam during the Vietnam War.

Below: This EC-121R acted as a
communications relay aircraft during air
strikes over North Vietnam and Laos.
Inset: The KC-135A tanker could be fitted
with a drogue attachment to refuel Navy and
Marine probe-equipped fighters.

with a TV guidance head which could be locked onto the target before launch and thereafter guide the bomb onto the aiming point. Another 'smart' munition was the laser-guided bomb which homed onto an aiming point which was designated by a laser illuminating pod carried by the strike aircraft. Both of these forms of guidance were fitted to 2000 and 3000lb bombs, making them ideal weapons for bridge busting. They were carried by the F-4s of the 8th TFW, which between 6 April and 30 June 1972 succeeded in destroying 106 bridges, including the repaired Paul Doumer bridge and the hitherto invincible Thanh Hoa Bridge.

While the fighter-bombers of the USAF were winging their way across southern Laos to attack North Vietnam from the west, to the east the attack carriers of the US Navy's Seventh Fleet were launching their air wings to attack the country from its seaward flank. Operating from Yankee Station in the Gulf of Tonkin there were often three carriers launching strikes on the North.

The composition of a carrier air wing varied somewhat according to the area of deployment and the size of the carrier (for example the *Essex* class were too small to operate the F-4 Phantom or A-6 Intruder). A typical air wing of the early war period was Air Wing 19 embarked on USS *Bon Homme Richard* (CVA-13) during a West Pacific cruise lasting from April 1965 to January 1966, which involved her in combat operations off Vietnam. The wing comprised two squadrons of F-8E Crusader air superiority fighters, two squadrons of A-4 Skyhawk light jet attack aircraft and a third attack squadron flying piston-engined A-1 Skyraiders. A photo reconnaissance detachment flew the RF-8 Crusader, while airborne early warning was provided by the E-1B Tracer and ECM escort by the EA-1F conversion of the Skyraider. Finally a squadron of UH-2A Seasprite helicopters was embarked for rescue and utility duties.

The LTV F-8 Crusader was a single-seat fighter powered by a 10,700lb thrust Pratt & Whitney J57 turbojet. Its maximum speed was Mach 1.8 at altitude, its service ceiling was 58,000ft and range was 1100 miles. Its armament comprised four 20mm Colt cannon with 100 rounds

of ammunition per gun, plus two or four AIM-9 Sidewinder missiles carried on the fuselage sides. For ground attack missions up to 5000lb of ordnance could be carried underwing. During the early years of the conflict Crusaders were the principal US Navy fighter aircraft in Vietnam and they are credited with destroying 19 North Vietnamese fighters. Losses however were heavy and between 1964 and 1973 83 Crusaders were destroyed.

The F-4B Phantom was the other important US Navy fighter of the conflict, and the later improved F-4J also saw combat service. Powered by two 17,000lb thrust J79 turbojets, the F-4B reached a maximum speed of 1485mph at 48,000ft, service ceiling was 62,000ft and range 800 miles. Its armament comprised four Sparrow and four Sidewinder air-to-air missiles and up to 16,000lb of bombs could be carried for strike missions. The F-4J had an improved radar and bombing computer. One of the highlights of the Phantom's US Navy career came on 10 May 1972. An F-4J of VF-96 flying from the USS *Constellation* (CVA-64) and crewed by Lt Randy Cunningham and Lt (jg) Willie Driscoll knocked down three MiG-17s in a single combat mission. As this crew had two earlier victories it made them the first American aces of the Vietnam War and as it turned out the only US Navy aces of the conflict.

Piston-engined Douglas A-1 Skyraiders saw service for the early years of the war from Navy carriers. However, as the North Vietnamese defenses improved they became increasingly relegated to missions in the less heavily-defended southern part of the country and in 1968 the type was withdrawn from service. The jet-engined A-4 Skyhawk fared much better. A single seat light attack aircraft, it was powered by a 8500lb Pratt & Whitney J52 turbojet, giving it a range of 700 miles and a maximum speed of 675mph at sea level. Its armament consisted of two 20mm cannon, each with 200 rounds of ammunition, mounted in the wing roots and up to 8200lb of ordnance carried on four underwing and a fuselage centerline pylons. The standard Navy light attack aircraft throughout the war, the A-4 flew more bombing missions than any other naval aircraft.

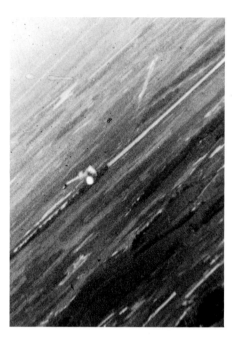

Above: An AIM-9 Sidewinder infra-red (heat-seeking) missile expodes on a MiG-17's jetpipe over North Vietnam.

The A-7A Corsair II was intended to replace the A-4, but in fact rather than superseding it the two types served on together. Powered by a 11,350lb thrust Pratt & Whitney TF-30 turbofan, the A-7A had a maximum speed of 679mph and a tactical radius of over 700 miles. Armament comprised two 20mm cannon and up to 20,000lb of ordnance. The A-7A first entered combat in December 1967 and was joined by the much improved A-7E in 1971, the new model having a more-efficient powerplant and navigation system and the M61 Vulcan multi-barrel cannon.

All-weather attack was the province of the two-seat Grumman A-6 Intruder, which first went into action in 1965. Powered by two 9300lb thrust Pratt & Whitney J52 turbojets, the A-6A had a maximum speed of 640mph and carried a bomb load of up to 18,000lb. Its sophisticated DIANE (Digital Integrated Attack Navigation Equipment) enabled it to find and attack small targets in all weathers, day or night. Its targets included bridges, power stations, barracks, military depots, railroad yards and fuel storage tanks. Lone Intruder missions were among the most successful bombing attacks on the North, one of their successes being the destruction of the Hai Duong bridge between Hanoi and Haiphong by a single A-6 of VA-65.

In addition to mounting fighter and attack missions, the air wings of the Seventh Fleet's carrier force undertook numerous valuable support tasks. Each carrier was a mobile tactical airfield, capable of carrying out reconnaissance missions using single-seat RF-8 Crusaders, or the vastly more sophisticated RA-5C Vigilante. This Mach 2 converted nuclear attack aircraft carried an extensive array of visual and electronic reconnaissance equipment, which included cameras, sideways-looking radar and electronic intelligence sensors. Airborne early warning aircraft, either the Gumman E-1 Tracer or the greatly advanced E-2 Hawkeye, not only defended the carrier task force from surprise attack, but also monitored the progress of strike forces

Above: A USAF strike force unloads its bombs on a railroad yard in North Vietnam, during the Rolling Thunder campaign.

Left: Rocket-armed attack aircraft from USS *Ranger*'s air wing attack North Vietnamese oil storage tanks.

over enemy territory, warning them of enemy interceptors. The strike force was not only protected by escort fighters, but also by the carrier's ECM jamming aircraft. Initially these were EA-1E Skyraiders and twin-jet EKA-3B Skywarriors, which combined the electronic warfare and air refuelling roles (another version of the Skywarrior, the RA-3B, was used for reconnaissance). Later and more capable electronic warfare aircraft were the EA-6A conversion of the Intruder and the four-seat EA-6B Prowler, which was also based on the Intruder design. The air wing's range of operational roles was completed by the UH-2 Seasprite and SH-3 Sea King rescue helicopters.

As already noted, the USAF, too deployed a wide range of support aircraft to enable its strike aircraft to operate effectively. From the spring of 1965 onward the strike force began to be opposed by enemy interceptors – at first MiG-17s and later MiG-19s and MiG-21s. Even a 1950s vintage MiG-17 could prove to be a dangerous opponent to a heavily bomb laden F-105 and so a MiG CAP escort began to accompany the strike force. This was generally provided by F-4

Top left: The AIM-9 Sidewinder air-to-air missile homed onto the hot exhaust of an enemy aircraft's powerplant.

Top right: The AIM-7 Sparrow AAM was a semi-active radar-guided missile, which required the launching fighter's radar to illuminate its target.

Above left: The AGM-85 Maverick air-to-ground missile was fitted with a TV guidance system, which was locked onto the target by the attack pilot before launch.

Above right: The AGM-78A Standard ARM homed onto enemy radar emissions.

Below: A Bullpup AGM streaks earthwards.

Phantoms, usually drawn from the 8th Tactical Fighter Wing in the early years of the war.

It was the 8th TFW, led by the indomitable Robin Olds – a P-51 Mustang ace of World War II – which mounted Operation Bolo in January 1967. This was an attempt to lure the enemy fighters into battle with the F-4s and it was to establish an ascendancy over the North Vietnamese Air Force which was never to be seriously challenged, although enemy interceptors continued to engage the strike aircraft right up until the end of hostilities. A formation of F-4s simulated a strike force of bomb-laden F-105s, inviting enemy interception. The North Vietnamese fell into the trap and the Phantoms had a field day, shooting down seven MiGs for no loss to themselves. Olds himself accounted for one of the enemy fighters, all of which were MiG-21s.

The North Vietnamese surface-to-air missiles (SAM), and anti-aircraft artillery proved to be as serious a menace to US strike aircraft as enemy interceptors. At first the enemy SAM sites were dealt with by 'Iron Hand' flights of bomb and missile armed F-100F fighters. Their defense suppression or Wild Weasel mis-

sion was one of the most dangerous activities of the air war. They were the first into the target area and the last out. Their job was to look for trouble and they often found it. An Iron Hand flight consisted of four fighters, F-100 in the early war years, later two-seat F-105Fs and the specialized Wild Weasel F-105G and, towards the end of the war, F-4 Phantoms. The aircraft were equipped with special warning receivers which enabled the backseater, always known as the Bear, to home in on a hostile ground radar emission. Once this was traced back to the SAM battery, a radar homing missile such as the Shrike or Standard ARM could be launched against the site, or it could be attacked with bombs or rockets. Generally two of the aircraft in an Iron Hand flight would carry anti-radiation missiles and the other two were armed with conventional ordnance.

Another effective counter to the North Vietnamese defenses was electronic countermeasures (ECM). The strike aircraft themselves carried ECM jamming pods which were effective against enemy radars, but they could only operate on preset frequencies and so were of limited flexibility. A more specialized ECM escort was required to gain the

maximum benefit from this jamming. The Douglas EB-66 Destroyer provided this essential support for most of the Vietnam conflict. A twin-engined bomber, powered by 10,000lb thrust Allison J71 turbojets, it was essentially the same design as the Navy's A-3 Skywarrior. Maximum speed was 594mph at 36,000ft and range was 1500 miles. As this performance was not really adequate for the EB-66 to accompany the strike force, it usually operated as a stand-off jamming system covered by its own escort of F-4s. The EB-66 carried a flight crew of three, plus four electronic warfare operators housed in a pressurized capsule fitted in place of the original aircraft's bomb bay.

Chaff – splinters of metallized foil – was an effective counter to enemy radars, as it blotted out all returns. However, its effect was of short duration and so tactics using this countermeasure had to be carefully timed and orchestrated. F-4 'chaff bombers' did not accompany the strike force until the Linebacker I and II campaigns of 1972.

At first they were used to sow a chaff corridor to and from the target, inside which the bombing aircraft could hide. However, this tactic was not entirely satisfactory, as it was found that the corridor tended to break down rather quickly as the chaff dispersed and the strike aircraft often strayed from the protection of the corridor. A preferred method was to sow a single, all-enveloping chaff cloud over the target. This too called for very accurate timing if it was to be effective and winds could dissipate the cloud too quickly.

The North Vietnamese defenses which the USAF strike forces had to defeat were equipped and trained along Soviet lines. The system comprised AA artillery, surface-to-air missiles and interceptor aircraft, plus an effective radar early warning and surveillance network. The AA defenses were formidable, com-

Below: According to North Vietnamese propaganda, this was a hospital bombed by B-52s during Linebacker II.

prising some 7000 guns of 37mm, 57mm, 85mm and 100mm caliber, many of them radar-controlled. It is estimated that these accounted for 68 per cent of American aircraft losses. There were some 200 SAM sites in North Vietnam during the period from 1967 until 1972 and these were armed with the SA-2 Guideline missile. Its effectiveness was not particularly high, as it was found to be susceptible to jamming and it could be evaded by a violent evasive maneuver. Yet even if the SA-2 was not a particularly effective weapon – and by 1972 over 150 SAMs were fired for every aircraft brought down – it did have an inhibiting effect on US air operations.

The North Vietnamese interceptor force was never very strong, presumably because of a lack of trained pilots. There is no evidence that Soviet or any other foreign 'advisors' flew combat missions over the North, as had happened in other postwar conflicts. In mid-1966 there were about 65 fighters in North Vietnam, about a dozen of them MiG-

21s and the remainder MiG-17s. By May 1972 the fighter force had increased to 200 aircraft, nearly half of which were MiG-21s and the remainder MiG-17s or Shenyang F-6s (the Chinese-built version of the MiG-19).

The most effective of these aircraft was the MiG-21, a Mach 2 short range interceptor armed with infra-red Atoll short-range missiles and a 23mm cannon. It was a highly maneuverable aircraft, as was the older MiG-17. The latter had a maximum speed of Mach 0.97 and was armed with three 23mm cannon. Perhaps the least effective of the trio was the MiG-19, which with a maximum speed of Mach 1.3 was slower than the MiG-21, but it had the agility which also made the MiG-17 such a dangerous opponent. The North Vietnamese interceptors operated under rigid ground control, thus following Soviet practice. However, in spite of the advantages of operating over their own territory, they never succeeded in dominating the air battles. During 1965-67 four

Above: A mixed formation of F-4Ds (OC tail code) and F-4Es (ED) serving with the 432nd TRW at Udorn in Thailand.
Below: An F-4E of the 388th Tactical Fighter Wing from Korat, Thailand, releases two 2000lb bombs.

MiGs were lost for every American fighter brought down, yet the exchange was a disappointment to American fighter pilots who had to live up to the tradition of 10 to 1 kill rates established during the Korean War.

Perhaps the most vital and least glamorous air mission of the Southeast Asia war was aerial refuelling. This role was primarily undertaken by Strategic Air Command's Boeing KC-135A Stratotankers, although the US Navy had their own tanker force of carrier-based KA-6Ds and EKA-3s, the Marine Corps flew the KC-130F and USAF air rescue helicopters refuelled from HC-130s. Virtually all tactical aircraft flying over North Vietnam required pre-strike and post-strike refuellings, as if they could rely on extra fuel when airborne they could then carry the maximum weapons load. Furthermore, the tactical fighters burned off a lot of fuel when maneuvering in full afterburner during combat and so often began their homeward flights at a dangerously low fuel state. B-52s operating from distant Guam also required tanker support to complete their mission.

The standard USAF air refuelling tanker used throughout the Vietnam war was the KC-135A, which was powered by four 13,750lb thrust Pratt & Whitney J57 turbojets. It had a maximum speed of 600mph and a range of 3000 miles. The usual crew complement was four, comprising pilot, co-pilot navigator and boom operator. The aircraft's total fuel capacity was 31,200 gallons, which could be transferred to another aircraft or used by the tanker itself in any proportion selected by the tanker's captain.

Fuel transfer was effected by means of a 46 feet extendable boom which was 'flown' by the boom operator into the receiver aircraft's receptacle. Once the connection was made, the fuel began to flow at a rate of almost 1000 gallons per minute. All that the receiver aircraft had to do was to find the tanker and position itself below and slightly behind it. This technique was much simpler from the receiver's point of view than the probe and drogue method used by US Navy and Marine aircraft and also by the USAF's HC-130s. This involved the tanker aircraft streaming a flexible fuel hose to which a drogue was attached. The receiver aircraft had to be flown so that its probe engaged the connection at the end of the tanker's hose before fuel could be transferred. This was a tricky process calling for skilled airmanship and could be even more difficult in turbulent air. A drogue attachment could be fitted to the KC-135A's boom to enable it to refuel probe equipped aircraft.

During the Southeast Asia conflict SAC's KC-135A Stratotankers flew 194,687 sorties and made 813,878 refuellings, transferring some 9 billion lbs of fuel in the process. Of the total number of sorties flown, 124,223 were in support of tactical air operations and the remainder to refuel SAC aircraft. While no tanker aircraft were lost to enemy action during the Southeast Asia war,

Below: RF-101C Voodoo tactical reconnaissance aircraft operated over Southeast Asia throughout the 1960s.

Above: Bombs are unloaded from a freighter at Guam to supply the B-52s based at Andersen AFB on the island.

four KC-135As were lost in operational accidents during this period.

Unlike the strike aircraft, whose activities were interrupted by bombing halts and circumscribed by 'no go' areas, the reconnaissance aircraft covered North Vietnam throughout the conflict. SAC's strategic reconnaissance aircraft – Lockheed U-2s and later Lockheed SR-71s – enjoyed the greatest immunity while operating over the North by virtue of their high altitude performance. The SR-71 flew at Mach 3 at altitudes above 80,000ft making it an impossible target for the North Vietnamese defenses. U-2s began operating over the North in 1965, providing details of the build-up of the air defenses. These sophisticated strategic reconnaissance aircraft – and especially the SR-71, as the U-2 was not totally immune from engagement by the SA-2 SAM – were found to be especially useful later in the conflict for monitoring the heavily defended Hanoi and Haiphong areas.

Strategic reconnaissance assets were

by no means readily available, as there were few U-2 and SR-71 aircraft in service and they had worldwide commitments quite apart from the needs of the Southeast Asia conflict. Consequently the day-to-day business of reconnaissance was carried out by tactical reconnaissance systems. The early tactical reconnaissance flights over the North were carried out by McDonnell RF-101C Voodoos. The Voodoo was a single-seat, twin-engined aircraft powered by two 14,500lb thrust Pratt & Whitney J57 turbojets. Performance included a range of some 2000 miles, a service ceiling of 45,000ft and a maximum speed of 875 knots. The RF-101C carried four cameras in the nose, which were interchangeable for day or night photography, plus two more in a fuselage bay. The Voodoo's performance was sufficient to deal with MiG-17 interceptors, which it could easily outrun. However, with the deployment of MiG-21s in 1967 the Voodoo lost it advantage and was redeployed for use over Laos and the South.

The Voodoo's successor was the Mach 2 RF-4C Phantom, a multi-sensor reconnaissance aircraft equipped with forward and sideways-looking radar, infra-

red sensor, plus vertical and oblique cameras. Combat radius was some 670 miles operating at high altitude, but this was reduced to just over 500 miles radius if the sortie had to be flown at low altitude. A great advantage of the RF-4C was that it had a sufficiently-good performance to allow it to accompany the strike force and photograph the results of an attack minutes after bomb release. However, a sufficient interval had to be allowed so that the smoke of exploding ordnance had cleared the target, but this was never so great as to deny the reconnaissance aircraft the protection of the strike force's fighter and ECM escorts.

Losses of manned reconnaissance aircraft over heavily defended areas were sometimes unacceptably high, for example in November 1967 two RF-4Cs were lost over Hanoi in as many days. For this reason the USAF developed unmanned reconnaissance drones for employment over such objectives. These high speed, low altitude pilotless craft, code named Buffalo Hunter, were modifications of Ryan-Teledyne target drones. They were carried beneath the wing of a Lockheed DC-130A drone launch and director aircraft and at the end of their mission the drones were usually recovered by a CH-3 helicopter. Yet although the drones were useful for covering high risk areas, they lacked the inherent flexibility of a manned aircraft. Manned reconnaissance missions involved a total of 650,000 sorties throughout the war.

An important support function in monitoring air strikes over the North and providing warnings of enemy fighter activity was carried out by Lockheed EC-121 aircraft operating under the code-name College Eye. These aircraft supplemented the coverage of ground-based radars and the US Navy's Crown early-warning ships so that a strike mission could be followed continuously from take-off until landing. The College Eye aircraft was also responsible for warning aircraft if they were about to stray into Chinese territory. Carrying early warning radar in prominent radomes above and below the fuselage, the EC-121 was powered by four 3250hp R-3350 engines which gave it a maximum speed of 320mph, a service ceiling just over 20,000ft and 4600 mile range.

From the viewpoint of aircrew

Below: High-flying Lockheed SR-71 'Blackbirds' monitored the build-up of North Vietnam's armed forces.

morale, perhaps the most significant support mission of the Southeast Asia conflict was air rescue. Over 3000 American and Allied airmen were recovered from the jungles of Southeast Asia during the war, and many of these were rescued under fire from under the noses of the enemy in the North. These rescues was not achieved without cost and the USAF's Aerospace Rescue and Recovery Service lost 45 aircraft and 71 aircrew killed in action during the course of the conflict.

The first rescue helicopter to be deployed to Vietnam was the Kaman HH-43 Huskie, a short range helicopter originally intended for dealing with aircraft crashes on or near its own air base. Clearly, the nature of the air war in Southeast Asia called for a longer-range helicopter, able to operate well away from its base and if necessary well into enemy terri-

tory. However, until more capable helicopters became available for the rescue mission, the Huskie had to cope with the air rescue demands of the conflict. Rescues at sea were undertaken by the Grumman HA-16 Albatross amphibian.

Various methods were used to extend the HH-43's operating radius, including installing extra fuel tanks in the Huskies and using forward operating bases in jungle clearing or remote mountain tops. Other modifications to the Huskie dictated by the conditions it met in Southeast Asia included the fitting of armor protection for the crew and installing a 250ft cable on the rescue hoist to facilitate rescues in dense rain forests. Powered by a single 825shp Lycoming T52 turboshaft, the Huskie had twin intermeshing rotor blades. Its top speed was 120 mph and range was about 230 miles.

The Huskie's successor was the

Above: A shot-down airman is winched aboard a USAF HH-53 Super Jolly Green Giant Rescue helicopter.

Below: The USAF's Aerospace Rescue and Recovery Service rescued over 3000 airmen from the jungles of Southeast Asia.

Sikorsky HH-3E, dubbed the Jolly Green Giant by American aircrew. It was powered by two 1400shp General Electric T58 turboshafts and had a maximum speed of 166mph and range of 625 miles. The HH-3E's range enabled it to reach any point in North Vietnam and return to base and its endurance could be further extended by in-flight refuelling from Lockheed HC-130 Hercules tanker aircraft. A still greater improvement in the equipment of the rescue units in Southeast Asia came with the introducton of the HH-53 Super Jolly Green Giant into service in 1967. This adaptation of the Marine Corps' Sea Stallion was a larger and more powerful rescue helicopter, capable of lifting a greater load than the HH-3E and able to counter groundfire with its three 7.62mm minigun rapid-fire machine guns. The HH-53s were also used to support Special Forces operations, notably the Son Tay prison camp rescue raid into North Vietnam in November 1970. A version of the helicopter designated CH-53 was specially developed for such tasks and it participated in the operations triggered by Cambodia's seizure of the American merchantman *Mayaguez* in May 1975.

The last American air operations over North Vietnam came as a result of the American mining of the important sea ports, which was finally authorized by President Richard Nixon in May 1972. A-6s from three carriers sowed mines in the harbors of Haiphong, Hon Gai, Cam Pha, Thanh Hoa, Vinh, Quang Khe and Dong Hoi, thus effectively sealing off North Vietnam from supplies by sea. As part of the January 1973 ceasefire agreement, the United States was responsible

for clearing these mines. Accordingly Task Force 78 was established to carry out the task, using minesweeping versions of the CH-53A Sea Stallion. The appropriately named Operation End Sweep ended in July 1973.

Above and below: The North Vietnamese Army's most potent air defense weapon was the Soviet-supplied SA-2 surface-to-air missile. In the later years of the Vietnam War there were some 200 SA-2 sites operational in the North.

NAVAL OPERATIONS

On the face of it there was no match between the respective navies of North Vietnam and the United States. A force of 18 ex-Chinese and ex-Russian motor torpedo boats and a motley collection of some 60 patrol craft and minesweepers was no match for the might of the US 7th Fleet. And yet it was not a conventional war which the US Navy would be called on to fight, and its ships, men and aircraft would be tested to the utmost in the campaign which started in 1964.

Although US Navy units were already stationed in the Gulf of Tonkin to keep track of coastal traffic taking arms and supplies from North Vietnam to the Viet Cong the initiative was taken by the North Vietnamese Navy. On the afternoon of 2 August, 1964 the destroyer *Maddox* (DD-731) was steaming in the gulf, outside the 12-mile limit, having completed a sweep to observe coastal movements. Suddenly three motor torpedo boats were sighted closing at high speed, and although warning shots were

Overleaf: The battleship USS *New Jersey* fires a salvo of 16in shells at a shore target in South Vietnam.

Below: Crewmen of a unit of the Vietnamese Junk Force search a fishing boat for contraband arms en route to the VC.

fired the strangers maintained course. When two torpedoes were seen to be fired the *Maddox* opened fire in earnest with her 5-inch guns, disabling one of her attackers and damaging a second. The torpedoes streaked by, an estimated 200 yards away, but in response to a call for the support, aircraft from the carrier *Ticonderoga* (CVA-14) were on the way, and as soon as they appeared the hostile MTBs sheered off.

The motive for this somewhat rash attack has never been established. The 7th Fleet had previously provided cover for South Vietnamese commando raids into North Vietnam, in which case the attack was simply retaliation for what the North Vietnamese regarded as unwarranted interference, or it may have been intended to embarrass President Johnson at the outset of his presidential campaign, but it did not have the desired effect, if that was the case. Lyndon Johnson refused to be drawn into immediate retaliation, and contented himself with warning the Hanoi government of the grave consequences which it faced if it ordered its forces to attack American warships.

Two days later there was a further incident, when the destroyer *Turner Joy* (DD-951) joined the *Maddox* on the Gulf

of Tonkin patrol. On the evening of 4 August both destroyers were steaming eastwards at about 20 knots when a radar operator aboard the *Maddox* reported what he identified as five small, fast targets approaching at a distance of about 36 miles. Both ships went to Battle Stations and opened fire with their 5-inch and 3-inch guns, and reported that they had sunk two motor torpedo boats and damaged two more.

Later, intelligence sources were to question the reaction of the destroyers, even claiming that the radar operator in the *Maddox* had mistaken the *Turner Joy's* high-speed wake for the 'blips' of motor torpedo boats. The fact remains that the two destroyer-captains thought that they had been attacked, and even more important, the US Government thought so too. The President ordered the carriers *Ticonderoga* and *Constellation* to deliver air strikes against four naval bases and a fuel depot in North Vietnam.

The attacks were claimed to have sunk 25 torpedo boats (clearly this must have included minor patrol craft) and set fire to 90 per cent of the oil fuel stocks in the

Right: A vessel of the Junk Force sails to intercept suspicious coastal craft.

country. Even if this estimate was true the cost was heavy: two US Navy planes shot down by ground AA fire and two damaged.

For a while the destroyer patrols in the Gulf of Tonkin (known as DESOTO operations) were suspended, and no incidents resulted, but as soon as they were resumed there was trouble. On the night of 18 September two destroyers, the *Parsons* (DDG-33) and *Morton* (DD-948) in the Gulf spotted on radar what they took to be hostile motor torpedo boats. Both ships took evasive action, and when after 40 minutes of maneuvering they had apparently failed to shake off their pursuers they opened fire with their 5-inch guns. The images disappeared from the radar screens, but twice more that night similar 'blips' appeared and before they finally stopped appearing the destroyers had fired more than 200 5-inch and 100 3-inch shells. No visual contact had been made and no torpedoes had been detected.

On such evidence the President was not prepared to authorize the bombing of North Vietnamese targets, and he tried to defuse the situation by suspending the DESOTO patrols once more.

Clearly, even if no attacks had been made people were getting jumpy, and a real engagement was highly likely.

For the moment all that was permitted by President Johnson was the discreet support of clandestine operations by South Vietnamese Navy units off the coast, designed to prevent arms and supplies from reaching the Viet Cong. Not until February 1965 was the US Navy permitted to launch any further air strikes, and then only after a provocative Viet Cong raid on American military advisers at Camp Holloway, near Pleiku. In all 49 fighter-bombers attacked a North Vietnamese Army barracks at Dong Hoi, just North of the Demilitarized Zone (DMZ). The US Navy's carriers and their air groups were the only way in which US military power could be brought to bear quickly, until USAF air bases could be established in South Vietnam. Even when the Air Force had sufficient aircraft to start Operation Rolling Thunder on 2 March, US Navy carrier aircraft continued to play an important role.

The heaviest strike aircraft used was the F-4B Phantom, a remarkable multi-role aircraft which could carry eleven

Above: A replenishment ship comes alongside the aircraft carrier USS *Oriskany*. Intensive air operations could empty a carrier's magazines of ordnance within three days.

Inset right: North Vietnamese motor gunboats pictured on patrol.

Right: The destroyer USS *Everett F. Larson* provides fire support for ARVN troops ashore with her five inch guns.

1000lb bombs or a mix of four Sparrow and four Sidewinder air-to-air missiles, had a maximum speed of nearly 1500mph and had a radius of 1000 miles in the ground attack role. It was capable of operating in all weathers, up to a ceiling of 71,000 feet. The Navy and Marine squadrons received their first F-4Bs in the early 1960s, over 200 of this type being followed by 260 F-4Js. The Phantom's combination of massive payload and high performance made it a good aircraft for the ground-attack role, but the smaller A-4 Skyhawk was available in much larger numbers, and so it saw wide service in Vietnam. Designed originally as a small daylight nuclear strike aircraft, the Skyhawk had by the early 1960s evolved into a versatile ground-attack aircraft. Its maximum speed was

670mph (without bombs, at sea level) and the payload was three 2000lb bombs or four Bullpup air-to-surface missiles (ASMs).

Good as these aircraft were, they were far outshone by the veteran A-1 Skyraider, a piston-engined aircraft which had seen service in Korea 15 years earlier, and had flown as a prototype in March 1945. Nicknamed the Spad in honor of the American Expeditionary Force's popular French biplane in World War I, the Skyraider could easily lift 8000lbs of ordnance, and is on record as having lifted nearly 15,000lbs on more than one occasion. Even more important was its ability to loiter over the target area, something which the thirsty jets could not do. The armament varied from two 20mm guns to tactical nuclear weapons, and no fewer than 15 hardpoints were provided for hanging ordnance under the wings. It is small wonder that out of the 3180 Skyraiders built, over 1000 were deployed in Southeast Asia.

At first Skyraiders suffered casualties from light anti-aircraft guns fired from jungle clearings. This turned out to a fault of the tactics employed; at medium altitude the aircraft was an easy target for machine guns and 20mm cannon. Only when the Skyraider pilots went lower, to tree-top height, did the aircraft realize its full potential; not only could it loiter and make follow-up attacks, but the noise of its 2700hp radial engine was a constant reminder to the enemy of its presence.

The Navy had, in addition to its Skyhawks and Phantoms, an excellent all-weather ground attack aircraft, the A-6 Intruder. Each carrier air wing also had four KA-6D tankers for in-flight refuelling, and there are in addition electronic warfare variants, the EA-6A Intruder and EA-6B Prowler. The basic version had a ceiling of nearly 45,000 feet and a maximum speed of 685mph. The payload was four Bullpup air-to-surface missiles (ASMs) or 13 1000lb bombs, or a combination of various weapons up to a total of 13,000lbs.

Reconnaissance is a prerequisite for efficient ground-attack, and all attack carriers were provided with photo-reconnaissance aircraft. The standard aircraft for this role was the RF-8G Crusader for US Navy squadrons, while the Marine squadrons received the RF-4B version of the Phantom (the standard F-8 Crusader was the principal daytime fighter aircraft until replaced by the F-4 Phantom). Backing up the photo-reconnaissance Crusaders and Phantoms were four squadrons of combined reconnaissance/heavy attack (RVAH) aircraft, RA-5C Vigilante bombers. These large multi-sensor aircraft carried their cameras, infra-red sensors and electronic countermeasures in a 'canoe' faired into the bottom of the fuselage, and four long-range fuel tanks hung under the wings, but if needed this payload could be replaced by bombs.

Like their USAF counterparts the Navy and Marine pilots had to face the North Vietnamese Air Force MiG-17,

MiG-19 and MiG-21 interceptors, as well as a growing weight of missile defense. The tactics needed to cope with sophisticated defenses belong to the story of the air war, but let it suffice that naval aircraft proved as good as land-based aircraft in coping with them.

An outstanding example of the sort of mission at which the Navy excelled was a raid on the railroad ferry across the Red River, in Hanoi, in October 1967. To stop the North Vietnamese ferrying rail-cars with war material across the Red River the USS *Constellation* launched a solitary A-6A Intruder, carrying 18 500lb bombs. The Intruder's mission was to destroy the loading slip for the rail ferry, a very small target to identify at night. As the plane flew low over the unfamiliar countryside it was attacked by a surface-to-air missile, about 18 miles from the target. Lt-Commander Hunter avoided the SAM by diving to rooftop height, and was able to dodge another 15 missiles while finding the target and destroying it.

Navy and Marine pilots took part in the 700 sorties flown against the Thanh Hoa Bridge, which spanned the Ma River about 80 miles south of Hanoi, but the bridge defied their efforts. Not even hits with Walleye TV-guided glide-bombs on the arches could bring the bridge down, and it was left to the USAF to achieve this feat, using laser-guided 'smart' bombs, six years later.

The US Marine Corps had pioneered the concept of vertical envelopment, using helicopters to deploy assault infantry far inland, and right from the start the helicopter was a vital element in the naval war. When the carriers were sent into the Gulf of Tonkin to lend support to Rolling Thunder a makeshift conversion of the SH-3A Sea King helicopters was authorized, increasing their fuel capacity and mounting 7.62mm Miniguns in their rear sponsons. Their task was to rescue shot-down pilots, and many heroic rescues were performed. By no means all the rescues were in jungle, for many damaged American aircraft came down in the Gulf, trying to get home after suffering damage from ground fire.

Then it could be a matter of reaching the pilot before an enemy junk.

When the United States took the momentous decision to become directly involved in Vietnam they had a formidable instrument of war to hand, the 125 ships and 64,000 men of the 7th Fleet, whose Task Group 77 (TF77) included the attack carriers *Hancock* (CVA-19), *Coral Sea* (CVA-43) and *Ranger* (CVA-61). Of these the *Hancock* was the oldest, having been commissioned as long ago as 1944, but she had completed a major modernization in 1956. This gave her all the post-1945 improvements, including steam catapults, an angled flight deck and landing sights. As her flight deck had been strengthened and the elevators enlarged the *Hancock* was capable of operating the latest aircraft, a mixed air group of 60-70 aircraft.

Below left: The attack carrier USS *Franklin D. Roosevelt* cruises in the Gulf of Tonkin in October 1966.

Inset below; The USS *White River* fires salvoes of rockets at VC targets ashore.

The *Coral Sea* displaced 52,500 tons (standard) as against the 33,100 tons of the *Hancock*, being one of three large 'battle carriers' completed after World War II. Her three acres of flight deck could operate up to 80 aircraft, using three steam catapults, and like the *Hancock* she operated a mix of strike, interceptor and reconnaissance aircraft. The *Ranger* was closer to the US Navy's idea of a modern carrier, having been built with her three sisters of the *Forrestal* class in 1952-59. They incorporated all the lessons of World War II, the Korean War and experience with jet aircraft, in a 1000ft long, 60,000-ton hull. The air group was a maximum of 90 aircraft, but the layout of the flight deck, with four steam catapults, enabled them to be used more efficiently than in the older CVAs.

TF77 was ordered to rendezvous on Yankee Station, 75 miles out in the Gulf of Tonkin, in December 1964, but at the start of February 1965 the *Hancock* and *Coral Sea* were ordered to rejoin the main 7th Fleet, as aggression against South Vietnam appeared to have been reduced. No sooner had the two carriers steamed away than the Viet Cong launched their attack on the American camp

at Pleiku, but such is the flexibility of sea power that they could be immediately returned to operational readiness, in time for the retaliatory strike, Operation Flaming Dart One. This began on 7 February, when 45 aircraft from the *Coral Sea* and *Hancock* bombed Dong Hoi Barracks. A strike by the *Ranger* on the same day against Vit Thu Lu had to be called off because of bad weather. In Flaming Dart Two, ordered after the destruction of a US barracks at Qui Nhon, carrier aircraft attacked a barracks at Chanh Hoa, 35 miles North of the DMZ. When Rolling Thunder started shortly afterward North Vietnam was divided into seven 'route packages', to be covered jointly by TF77 and the US 7th Air Force.

Looking back on the best part of two decades it is important to remember how strict the Pentagon's rules of engagement were. Each target had to be authorized from Washington, and furthermore each mission was individually approved. Follow-up attacks were not permitted, and hostile aircraft had to be positively identified.

The surface naval forces had a more humdrum task, but it was of equal im-

Above: An RA-5C Vigilante reconnaissance aircraft prepares to catapult from the attack carrier USS *Coral Sea*.

Right: A CH-53A tows its minesweeping 'sled' through the waters of Haiphong Harbor during clearance operations in 1973.

Inset right: The South Vietnamese Navy's HQ Ngoc Hoi (formerly USS *Battleboro*) prepares for her first cruise.

portance. As early as February 1965 it was known that North Vietnamese ships were running large quantities of munitions into South Vietnam. The answer was a tight blockade of the coast, with surveillance centres set up at An Toi, Da Nang, Nha Trang, Qui Nhon and Vung Tau. Under 7th Fleet control a Vietnam Patrol Force, Task Force 71 was established. Operation Market Time was made the responsibility of this force, the counterpart of the riverine Game Warden. The main task was to maintain an inspection patrol to monitor the movements of junks, but as there were about 1000 each day there was only an outside chance of identifying a clandestine craft carrying supplies to the Viet Cong. The first ships sent for this purpose were half a dozen radar picket destroyer escorts

(DERs) released from radar picket duty in the North Atlantic and Pacific, an unlikely choice for the job. However the DERs had long endurance as well as good radar and communications, with a useful light armament in case they were attacked. They had sufficient accommodation on board to be able to provide relief crews, food, water and fuel for the smaller patrol craft, and so they were virtually HQ ships for the offshore force.

An even more useful reinforcement was Coast Guard Squadron One, with its *Swift* type 50ft patrol boats. They had an armament of twin .50 cal. machine guns above the deckhouse, and a combined .50 cal. machine gun and 81mm mortar aft. The *Swift* design had started life as an aluminium-hulled utility boat, but it proved ideal for coastal surveillance. They were crewed by an officer and five enlisted men, who lived ashore or on board larger ships and an eventual total of 104 was ordered. Also available were 26 of the Coast Guard's 83ft cutters, painted dark gray to reduce visibility at night.

More specialized craft were also introduced, notably the 164-ft *Asheville* (PG-84) class patrol gunboats. These novel aluminum craft were driven by a combination of diesels and gas turbines at a maximum speed of 50 knots. With such high speed, a draught of less than 7ft and an armament of a single rapid-fire 3-inch gun and a 40mm Bofors gun they were formidable antagonists but they proved rather over-complex for the task. Also too sophisticated for the job was the experimental hydrofoil *Tucumcari* (PGH-2), which was soon sent home.

It was quickly obvious that surveillance operations were more effective with the assistance of patrol aircraft, and by the end of 1965 there were P-5 Marlin seaplanes operating from tenders and land-based P-3A Orion maritime patrol aircraft available. The Marlins patrolled from Vung Tau down to Phu Quoc Island off the southern coast of Cambodia, while the Neptunes operated north of Vung Tau up to the 17th Parallel, but later the seaplanes were replaced by P-2 Neptunes flying from Tan Son Nhut, Saigon and eventually Cam Ranh Bay and Thailand.

No description of the naval war in Vietnam would be complete without mention of the US Marine Corps, who used their unique experience in amphibious warfare to outflank the Viet Cong and the North Vietnamese Army. At the beginning of 1965 the 9th Marine Expeditionary Brigade (MEB) in transports of Task Force 76 had been held in readiness off South Vietnam. The two battalions were ordered ashore to protect Da Nang air base, and both were in position by 12 March, taking only five days to deploy. A third battalion went ashore near Da Nang on 10 April, allowing two companies to be lifted by helicopter to Phu Bai, 42 miles to the northwest. By the end of that month nearly 9000 Marines were established ashore.

At the beginning of May 1965, 9th MEB was expanded to become 3rd Marine Amphibious Force (MAF), with three more battalions, and by the middle of the month they had been joined by another battalion, bringing the total up to seven. There were now an artillery regiment in support, and the first elements of the 1st Marine Aircraft Wing. The first land-based Marine Phantoms flew from Da Nang on 6 May, and soon there were four Marine Air Groups (MAGs), two operating fixed-wing aircraft and two equipped with helicopters. A novel development was the building of a Short Airfield for Tactical Support (SATS) at Chu Lai. This was achieved by laying a 4000ft airstrip of aluminium matting, complete with arrestor wires, just like an aircraft carrier. It was even possible to provide a catapult, although this was not installed for another two years, and until then the aircraft had to rely on rocket-assisted takeoff. Even more remarkable was the fact that the Chu Lai SATS was built in 24 days.

On 12 May the Rolling Thunder air raids were suspended as a peace overture, but two days later the Navy was given permission for the first time to bombard shore positions. Initially gunfire support was provided by destroyers, for very few of the 6-inch and 8-inch gunned cruisers were in commission, and it was soon clear that the 5-inch gun lacked the range and weight of shell to provide effective support. The relatively small number of 5-inch guns was limited; the older *Gearing* class destroyers were armed with two twin 6-inch/38 mountings, whereas the newer

Above: USS *New Jersey* bombards targets near Tuyhoa in the Central coastal region of South Vietnam in March 1969.

Forrest Sherman (DD-931) class had only three of the newer 5-inch/54 guns and the big missile-armed destroyer leaders of the *Coontz* class carried only one gun.

In response to increasing calls from the Marines for heavy gunfire support, a number of cruisers were sent to join the 'Gun Line'. One of the biggest, the *Newport News* (CA-148) had been serving as flagship of the Second Fleet in the Atlantic, but on 5 September 1967 she left Norfolk, Virginia for the long haul across the Pacific, via the Panama Canal. By 9 October she was ready to open fire, as part of Operation Sea Dragon, a concerted effort to interrupt the flow of supplies across the DMZ. Ironically it was the first time that the 17,000-ton cruiser had fired her guns in anger, in 19 years of service, and by the time she completed her 226 days of duty on 18 April, 1968 she had fired 59,000 shells of various calibers. A second tour of duty lasted from December 1968 to June 1969, but a third tour started in late 1971 was interrupted by an accidental explosion in one of her triple 8-inch turrets. According to the official Navy communique the explosion destroyed the center barrel of No 2 turret. The normal powder charge was

loaded for the fourth round of the fire mission, but as soon as it was fired the shell exploded in the barrel, starting a fire in the turret and killing all 16 crewmen instantly. The entire forward part of the ship was engulfed in smoke, and subsequently it was discovered that another three sailors died from the effects of the smoke.

The *Newport News* was ordered to Subic Bay in the Philippines for repairs but she was so valuable on the Gun Line that no attempt was made to replace the damaged gun. Instead she returned to action with the center gunport sealed off, and the turret unuseable. Until the commissioning of the battleship *New Jersey* she had the heaviest punch, being able to drop a 335lb shell on a target 14 or 15 miles away.

What the Marines really wanted was the maximum gunfire support, and that could only be provided by recommissioning a battleship. In mid-1967 the 51,000-ton *New Jersey* (BB-62) was stripped for overhaul, and after the expenditure of $21 million was ready for duty the following April. Apart from general refurbishing and replacement of defective wiring, the alterations were

confined to stripping out the scores of light anti-aircraft guns and providing her with an up-to-date suite of communications gear. The communications overhaul was absolutely vital to allow the ship to cooperate with other warships as well as land and air units.

Amid an upsurge of nostalgia the *New Jersey* left for the Western Pacific in 1968. She proved her worth by spending a total of 120 days on the Gun Line, 47 of them continuously at sea. Before the end of the commission she fired a total of 5688 16-inch shells in action, as well as 15,000 rounds from her battery of 5-inch secondary guns. By comparison she had fired only 771 16-inch shells during her first commission, in World War II and 6671 shells during the Korean War. After such a tremendous effort to get a battleship out to Vietnam it is all the more surprising that she was decommissioned in December 1969. Part of the problem was the acute shortage of skilled manpower caused by the mobilization of so many other Navy ships, but the

Below: A battle-damaged A-4 Skyhawk engages the crash barrier of USS *Oriskany* on its return from an air strike.

Top: The accidental firing of an F-4's Zuni rocket caused this fire on USS *Forrestal*'s flight deck in July 1967.

Above: The smaller US carriers, such as USS *Bennington*, could not operate heavy aircraft such as the F-4 and RA-5C.

Marine Corps was particularly vociferous in opposing the withdrawal of the *New Jersey*.

In answer to the question of vulnerability, not only of a battleship but all the other Gun Line ships off the coast of Vietnam, individually all the older warships were vulnerable to air attacks from the North Vietnamese Air Force. However, with the carriers in the vicinity it was possible to provide a Combat Air Patrol (CAP) over the Gun Line, backed up by air defence ships, missile-armed destroyers and destroyer leaders (DDGs and DLGs) and cruisers (CGs and CLGs). The air defence ships were stationed in a Positive Radar Advisory Zone (PIRAZ) in the Gulf of Tonkin. In 1972 the heavy cruiser *Chicago* (CG-11) played a major role in supporting the airborne mining of Haiphong harbour. Her task was to cover the critically timed, vulnerable low-level mining operations. As the heavily laden aircraft approached the entrance to Haiphong the cruiser detected MiGs on her radar, heading to intercept. She fired a salvo of

Talos long-range surface-to-air missiles, knocking down one MiG at a range of 48 miles and forcing the others to turn away. Thereafter the mining mission was unopposed.

Shortly afterwards the *Chicago* distinguished herself again. While operating on the PIRAZ station one of her air controllers directed Air Force and Navy fighters to no fewer than 12 MiG kills. During 1972 MiGs only attempted to penetrate the PIRAZ 'umbrella' once, and that attack was broken off when the destroyer leader *Biddle* (CG-34) destroyed one of the attack-leaders. Missile ships were on continuous Search and Rescue missions because they could provide missile defence over vast areas, operate their own helicopters and at the same time control the teams of attack and fighter aircraft and the rescue helicopters. Missile ships were also used to fire Anti Radiation Missiles (ARM) to home on hostile radar transmissions and destroy missile guidance systems ashore.

On 1 August, 1965 the growing tempo of the naval war was reflected in a change of command. Responsibility for the Market Time operation was removed from the 7th Fleet. A new Task Force 115, the Coastal Surveillance Force was created under Rear Admiral Norvell G Ward, who was also Chief of the Naval Advisory Group. On 18 December Task Force 116, the River Patrol Force, was hived off, although it and its Game Warden operations remained under the command of Rear Admiral Ward. On 1 April 1966 the whole operation was upgraded when Admiral Ward was appointed Commander, Naval Forces, Vietnam (COMNAVFORV).

It is impossible to list all the Navy ships which served in Vietnam but certain highlights stand out. In December 1965 the carrier *Enterprise* (CVAN-65) arrived on station, the first nuclear-powered aircraft carrier to see active service. One of the more incongruous sights of the war was her giant flight deck covered with piston-engined A-1 Skyraiders, being ferried to Vietnam. Her arrival coincided with an official announcement that Navy and Marine pilots had

logged 56,888 sorties over Vietnam. In February 1966 the first aerial mining operations were begun, in an attempt to interdict the movement of supplies by sea. On 25 October the Navy began Operation Sea Dragon, in parallel with the Rolling Thunder offensive. The purpose was to disrupt coastwise traffic, but under strict rules of engagement.

The intensity of flying operations meant an inevitable increase in aircraft losses, but the carriers themselves began to suffer casualties. In August 1966 a magnesium flare was fired accidentally aboard the carrier *Oriskany*, and in the fire which followed 44 crewmen died and 38 were injured. On 29 July, 1967 the carrier *Forrestal* (CVA-59) suffered a much worse accident, when a rocket projectile was fired accidentally. The explosion started a fire which lasted 18 hours, and by the time it was extinguished 21 aircraft had been destoyed and 134 crewmen were dead. The ship was extensively damaged and required a seven-month repair in the United States.

On the advice of the Commander in

Chief, Pacific (CINCPAC) Admiral Sharp there was a redefinition of targets in 1967. Priority was to be given to electrical power, war support industry, transportation and support, military complexes, fuel storage and missile defences. On CINCPAC's advice some of the restrictions on targets was lifted, but for the most part the Pentagon continued to select targets on a piecemeal basis. In February 1968 carrier pilots had to fly 1500 sorties in support of the beleagured Marines at Khe Sanh, followed by 1600 in March, before the siege was finally lifted.

In February 1969 the colossal task of Vietnamization began, with the first riverine and coastal patrol craft turned over to the South Vietnamese Navy. Within a year virtually all the Game Warden and Market Time craft had been transferred or sent home, although March also saw the last large-scale action

Below: Two Swift boat sailors man the vessel's 'over-and-under' weapon – a combination of 0.50mg and 81mm mortar.

32 Landing Craft, Medium
(LCMs)
10 light monitors
53 Landing Craft, Vehicle and
Personnel (LCVPs)
over 300 minor craft, including a
training ship, 2 oilers and various
supply craft

Above: A US Navy inshore patrol craft
makes a high-speed run off the coast of South
Vietnam in February 1969.

fought by the Marines. Forces of the 3rd
MAF fought Operation Dewey Canyon
in the Da Krong valley in Quang Tri
Province, inflicting heavy casualties and
capturing much ammuntion.

According to the records the last US
Navy fighting forces left in Vietnam
were the men and aircraft of Light
Attack Squadron 4, which left on 1
April, 1971. They were flying the OV-10
Bronco, a remarkable aircraft designed
specifically for Counter Insurgency
(COIN) duties. It was a twin piston-
engined aircraft capable of flying slowly
over the battle area, and having good
downward visibility to allow observation
of ground targets and to allow the pilot
to mark targets with precision. The
Broncos had originally been given to
the Marines in 1968, and had the war
gone on they might have had the chance
to prove their worth, but the provision of
such specialized equipment was coming
too late to affect the outcome. In mid-
April the headquarters of III MAF, the
1st Marine Division and the 1st Marine
Aircraft Wing left Da Nang, leaving
only the 3rd Marine Amphibious Brigade. After US ground and air operations stopped on 7 May the exodus of
American military personnel increased,
and when 3rd MAB left at the end of July
the only Marines left in the country were
a few advisers and embassy guards.

The 'withdrawal of the legions' did
not, of course, end the war. The South
Vietnamese Navy had received a total of
242 patrol craft in 1969, making it,
numerically at least, one of the larger
navies. It already possessed a formidable
force:

2 640-ton PCE type escorts
4 650-ton MSF type escorts
2 280-ton PC type patrol craft
26 95-ton PGM type motor
gunboats
3 320-ton MSC type coastal
minesweepers
3 Tank Landing Ships (LSTs)
7 Landing Ships, Medium (LSMs)
7 Landing Ships Support, Large
(LSSLs)
5 Landing Ships Infantry, Large
(LSILs)
7 Landing Craft, Utility (LCUs)

Most of these vessels had been transferred direct from the US Navy, but
some had originally been transferred to
France as long ago as 1951. In addition
there was a coastal force of 500 moto-
rized junks, established with American
assistance on 12 April, 1960. From an
initial strength of 100 the force was
rapidly expanded, and by the middle of
1962 there were 28 patrol groups operating. Armament was limited to .50 cal
and .30 cal machine guns and later junks
were fitted with bullet-proof plating.

The Junk Force was strengthened by
the construction of new craft, with the
benefit of new technology – fiberglass
was used to protect their bottom plank-
ing from marine borers, the traditional
enemy of wooden hulls. Until July 1965
the Junk Force was a para-military
force, but thereafter it was put under
naval control. By mid-1967 it was manned by 4000 men. The Junk Force was
subsequently reduced by the elimination
of the older sailing types. By the beginning of 1972 there were only 246, broken
down into 62 command junks, 31 of the
Kien Giang type and 153 of the Yabuta
type. Some of the Yabuta type were built
of ferro-concrete.

In 1972, after the Americans had pulled out, the South Vietnamese Navy was
swollen by the transfer of all the minor
craft already mentioned, but there were
in addition many major warships, and
personnel had risen to 40,275 officers
and enlisted men, and 13,800 marines.
The largest ships were seven ex-US
Coast Guard cutters, 311-ft long and
armed with a 5-inch gun and one or two
81mm mortars and machine guns. These
useful 1750-ton ships had been built in
World War II as seaplane tenders of the
Barnegat class, and had been transferred
to the Coast Guard in 1946-48.

The value of the radar picket destroyer escorts has been mentioned ear-

Below: Two of the major units of the US Navy's Seventh Fleet sail in company – USS *New Jersey* and USS *Coral Sea*.

lier, and two DERs, the USS *Camp* (DER-251) and *Forster* (DER-334) became HQ★ *Tran Hung Dao* and *Tran Khanh Du* in 1971. They displaced 1590 tons (standard) and were armed with two single 3in anti-aircraft guns, a Hedgehog anti-submarine mortar and two sets of triple anti-submarine torpedo-tubes. Their twin-shaft diesels drove them at 21 knots and they were manned by 170 men. Much of the top-secret electronic warfare equipment was removed before the transfer, but they retained their AN/SPS-28 and AN/SPS-10 surveillance radars. Both ships had originally been built as anti-submarine escorts for the Battle of the Atlantic in World War II, and had been converted to radar picket duties in the 1950s.

It would be wrong to assume that withdrawal of ground troops and land-based aircraft had reduced the burden on the US Navy. Right up to the end of 1972 shore bombardments were carried out in support of ARVN operations. In May of that year President Nixon ordered the mining of Haiphong and other North Vietnamese harbors, in response to repeated calls to stop the supply of Soviet weapons. Such was the sophistication of these mines that the United States would subsequently take responsibility for sweeping them, using helicopters to tow 'sleds' specially fitted to counter the various types of fuzing.

Inevitably the US Navy had to play a major role in the evacuation which followed the final debacle in April 1975. Carriers and amphibious warfare ships such as the USS *Blue Ridge* had to find space for frantic refugees. At one time so many South Vietnamese helicopters were trying to land on board that some had to be pushed overboard to make room – a dreadful comment on the waste and futility of war. Some tens of thousands of refugees were picked up by US Navy ships, and others reached Thailand after voyages of unbelievable hardship in open boats. Long afterwards these 'boat people' continued to risk their lives on the high seas, and the total number who died in the attempt will never be known.

★All South Vietnamese ship-names were prefixed by HQ, for *Hai Quan* (= Navy).

After such a tale of disaster and defeat, the final involvement of the US Navy in South-East Asia was remarkably successful. On 12 May 1975 Cambodian forces seized the American merchant ship SS *Mayaguez* while she was *en route* to Thailand. It was a classic problem: the US forces were strong enough to capture the ship, but until the whereabouts of the captain and his crew of 39 could be ascertained the rescuers would have to proceed with great caution.

While warships, including the attack carrier *Coral Sea* headed at full speed for the Gulf of Thailand aircraft kept a watch over the stationary *Mayaguez*, forcing back or sinking any boats near the ship. All available helicopters were despatched to U-Tapao Air Base in Thailand, with USAF security police and Marines flown in from Okinawa.

The first part of the rescue went badly wrong when an Air Force helicopter crashed, killing all 23 people on board. Nor did the second part go much better, when eight CH-53 helicopters tried to land the Marines at Koh Tang, on the Cambodian coast near the *Mayaguez*. Intelligence reports indicating that Koh Tang was defended by 150 to 200 Cambodians armed with heavy weapons had not reached U-Tapao. No sooner had the first CH-53 landed than a hail of small arms, rocket and mortar fire was unleashed. The pilot managed to lift the big helicopter off on one engine, but it fell into the sea. The second CH-53 was also badly hit but drew clear with its

Above: Marine security guards escort refugees aboard USS *Hancock* after the fall of Saigon in April 1975.

Marines still on board and struggled back to Thailand. A third helicopter was hit in an engine and came down on the beach, but the fourth burst into flames before landing, killing 13 men. The fifth offloaded her Marines but returned to Thailand with severe damage, and only the last three helicopters were able to land their Marines after some hours.

Fortunately the destroyer escort *Harold E Holt* (DE-1074) was nearby, and a further three CH-53 helicopters landed their Marines on board. From there they were able to capture the abandoned *Mayaguez* without difficulty. Then came the welcome news that the captain and crew had been found ashore, where they had been turned loose by their captors, and a boat was sent to pick them up. It remained only to get the Marines away from Koh Tang, who were in great danger. To prevent Cambodian aircraft from hindering the rescue an air strike was launched from the *Coral Sea* against Ream airfield, and Koh Tang was then attacked by helicopter gunships and aircraft. Finally after nightfall the last Marines were lifted out by helicopter, under covering fire.

In retrospect the *Mayaguez* affair was a 'close-run thing' which had all the hallmarks of hasty planning and poor intelligence. But it succeeded, and quickly, unlike the similar *Pueblo* capture off North Korea seven years earlier. By its firm and rapid counteraction the Pentagon showed the world that in spite of the defeat in South Vietnam the United States was still prepared to protect its interests.

The naval lessons of the ten-year war are difficult to assess. In one sense the US Navy was simply going along with a strategy already determined by politics and the existing state of affairs, and it could not be blamed for the fundamental errors in the direction of the war. On the other hand its forces had acquitted themselves very well in reacting to the peculiarities of riverine war, especially when it is borne in mind that the US Navy had until 1965 had only minimal light forces. The development of specialized river monitors and assault craft showed great ingenuity, and did a great deal to delay defeat.

Like the land and air forces, the Navy had been equipped to fight high technology warfare, and this proved ill-suited to the sort of war that was being waged in Vietnam. The despised gun was found to be much more useful than anyone had imagined, and several of the all-missile ships hurriedly shipped obsolescent 5-inch and 3-inch guns in any available space, not to defend themselves but to strengthen the Gun Line. Despite its unequalled record of amphibious assault in the Pacific in World War II there had been declining interest in gunfire support in the Navy, and the fire control equipment was not particularly efficient in this role. Nor did the current model of 5-inch gun, the 54 cal. Mk 42, prove as reliable as the older 5-inch/38 cal. twins and singles of World War II vintage.

Although the missile-armed cruisers and destroyers scored several kills against hostile MiGs, particularly during the later years of the war, no ships were hit. This may have led to a false sense of security, for in effect the naval forces seem to have enjoyed the same sort of 'sanctuary' granted tacitly by the North Koreans in the Korean War. Although there were occasional duels between ships and shore artillery, and some attempts to penetrate the Fleet's air defenses, the North Vietnamese do not appear to have made any concerted effort to attack US naval forces. Even the original attack on the destroyers in the Gulf of Tonkin back in 1964 is open to

doubt, as it may have been an erroneous reading of intentions. One can hardly avoid the conclusion that even if the North Vietnamese had wished to score a humiliating reverse against the navy, their Russian paymasters would almost certainly have vetoed it on the grounds that it would have been too provocative. What is certain is that if the Soviets had wanted the North Vietnamese to try out some of their anti-ship missiles, for example, these weapons would have been supplied without any hesitation.

Ironically one of the most important lessons for the US Navy and for other Western navies was caused by accident. In 1973 the missile frigate USS *Worden* (DLG-18) was operating off the coast when an F-4 Phantom flying high overhead accidentally released a Shrike anti-radiation missile. The missile armed itself and performed exactly as intended, homing on the DLG's main surveillance radar and detonating about 80ft overhead. Its blast and fragmentation warhead severed all topside waveguides and cable leads, and the wheelhouse was extensively damaged. All electrical power was lost, and for some six hours the ship was effectively out of action as a fighting unit, although from a short distance away she seemed undamaged.

The extent of damage from such a small warhead was alarming enough, but on close examination it was found that the aluminum superstructure itself had contributed even more to the damage.

Blast had shattered aluminum panels and flung fragments around the wheelhouse, and every splinter from the missile had produced two or more 'shotgun pellets' – in all some 60 per cent of the damage to the *Worden* was attributed to the aluminum structure, rather than the Shrike's warhead. Since then damage to British ships in the Falklands has confirmed the *Worden* findings, and in the latest American warships much more attention is paid to splinter protection of the superstructure; the newest destroyers will have an all-steel structure.

In various ways the Vietnam War had a profound effect on the US Navy. Traditional techniques and weapons were to a great extent vindicated, and several assumptions about the newer technology were called into question. On the other hand, all the latest ships, aircraft and weapons were tested and proved reliable. One of the least publicized successes of the entire war was the very high level of mechanical reliability of ships' machinery – many ships spent three or four months at sea without respite, and crews proved adept at carrying out major repairs themselves, with little or no base support. Above all, officers and men were given invaluable experience of war conditions, making the US Navy the most combat-experienced navy in the world.

Below: A CH-53 helicopter flies refugees onto the deck of USS *Hancock* from Saigon during the evacuation of the city.

INDEX

ACKNOWLEDGMENTS

Associated Press 8-9, 125
Robert Hunt Picture Library 9, 20-1, 48, 61, 68, 88-9, 90, 91, 94/5, 100(2), 105, 132, 137
Remington Arm Company 32
United States Air Force 2-3, 6-7, 106-7, 108, 109(2), 110-1, 110, 112(3), 114(2), 115, 116-7, 117(2), 118-9, 119, 120(4), 124, 125, 126, 127, 151, 152-3, 154-5, 156(2), 157, 159(3), 162-3, 162, 164, 165, 166-7
United States Army 4-5, 11, 13, 14, 15(2), 16, 18, 19, 20, 22-3, 26-7, 28, 29, 30(2), 31, 32, 33, 34, 35(2), 36-7, 37, 40(2), 49, 57, 65, 68-9, 71, 73, 74-5, 76(2), 77, 80, 81, 84, 86-7, 136, 141
United States Department of Defense 35(2), 38, 39(2), 44, 46-7, 50-1, 51(2), 54(3), 55, 56, 58-9, 58, 60, 63(2), 64, 66-7, 71, 72(2), 74, 75, 78-9, 79, 82, 83, 85(3), 86-7, 91
United States Marine Corps 12, 13, 17, 23, 98, 150, 188, 189
United States Navy 41, 52-3, 56-7, 122-3, 128-9, 130-1, 131, 132-3, 134-5, 136(2), 137, 138, 139, 140, 142-3, 144, 145(2), 146(2), 147(2), 148(2), 149, 168, 170-1, 172, 173, 174, 175(2), 176, 177, 178, 179(2), 180, 182(2), 184, 185(2), 186-7
Government of Vietnam 9, 24, 25(3), 44-5, 91, 92, 93(3), 96, 97, 98, 101(2), 102(2), 160, 161